ART and SPACE

ROCHERS DANS LE PARC DU CHATEAU NOIR. CEZANNE

ART and SPACE

by

AARON BERKMAN

SOCIAL SCIENCES PUBLISHERS

NEW YORK

Acknowledgments to Carol Tomberg for aid in rendering the drawings and Dr. Maurice J. Shore for encouragement in bringing this work to completion; Victoria Berkman, Ruth Siler and Moses Berkman for general assistance.

PRINTED IN THE UNITED STATES OF AMERICA

Table of Contents

List of Plates

List of Figures

Preface

TO THE AVERAGE OBSERVER CONTEMPORARY ART SEEMS TO BE in a state of confusion. As he surveys the field he finds paintings which represent every style, from the ethnographic primitive and the historically traditional to the impressionist, as well as some that are completely strange and bear no resemblance to anything he has ever known. Furthermore, the different co-existing tendencies are pulling against each other, every school proclaiming its own products the only true ones.

Actually, art functions to portray life in its many manifestations. Some contemporary painters attempt to do this through the well established techniques developed in the past. Others find them inadequate for the interpretation of the knowledge and orientation of our times, and are experimenting with a new pictorial language capable of containing our expanding horizons.

Our knowledge has increased enormously within the last one hundred years. Early science was confined to that which could be seen, touched and tasted. But since the discovery of bacteria, nuclear radiation, the theory of relativity and the existence and activities of the sub-conscious mind, science has invaded territories which lie beyond our sensory perceptions and can be apprehended only through the correlation of certain phenomena.

9

This being a reality of modern life, the artist today is looking for a corresponding symbol with which to express it. There is nothing new about his attempt. Primitive art, for instance, which seems to us purely abstract, was originally a symbolic manner of expressing the thoughts and feelings of primitive man. It is abstract to us only when we have no key to decipher it.

Art, philosophy and science always parallel each other. They are three different ways of exploring facts and realities. A study of the history of art and of the general intellectual life in any given period invariably reveals corresponding tendencies in all fields, the one serving as a key to an understanding of the others. The development of the theory and techniques of spacial organization in painting, for instance, reflects throughout history an equivalent development in scientific knowledge and philosophical thinking.

To illustrate, let us think for a moment of the great periods in history and of their art:

In the Middle ages, religion was the focal point of the intellectual and emotional life in the West. The factual conditions of earthly existence were a negligible value, and nature was merely the setting for the spiritual life of man. Medieval art is therefore concerned solely with religious subjects, where forms are arranged in the order of their importance without regard for optical truth.

The Renaissance inaugurated the scientific age. Medicine and mathematics occupied the best minds and intellects. The individual, in relation to religion and society, became important and a subject of art. Renaissance art developed the theory of perspective and, while still concerned with religion, placed the emphasis on the human element. The figures were conceived in the grand manner, in keeping with the romantically aristocratic attitude of the time.

In the 19th century the development of photography and the application of the prism of light has its equivalent in Impressionism, where objects were painted as they appeared in a moment of time and color was broken down into its primary components.

The great art of all these periods survives because it is a true interpretation of its times, and despite changing values it is still valid for us because of its universality in spirit.

However, when it comes to modern art the general public is confused. While it accepts the largely "mysterious" findings of the scientists, and zestfully debates the various current systems of philosophy, it refuses to accept the more unusual forms of modern art and still clings to the models of the past. "To discern a form is to verify a preexisting idea," says Albert Gleizes; and the public is reluctant to accept the existence of new ideas in art.

Yet, abstract and non-objective painting is as logical a continuation of the past as modern science. The contemporary artist, equipped with the technical knowledge of his forebears and the advance theories of today, feels free to travel along uncharted roads. The key to modern art may therefore be a study of the basic artistic techniques and their development. Since some contemporary artists create forms in the heat of their enthusiasm which they themselves find it difficult to explain afterwards, such a study may also be the only way to weed out that which is merely obscure and evasive and attempts to pass for profundity.

This book is given to the study of space in art. This problem, the various systems employed for its solution, as well as their relationship to science will be expounded and illustrated.

The ideas presented here are not necessarily new. Medieval space, the mathematics of perspective, Cezanne's innovations and modern theories have been discussed in other works. This volume attempts to explore the pattern of growth from the earliest system to the present.

Space organization as a subject is possibly the most basic technical problem in the study of painting. Many books on composition have misfired because they consider pictorial design as the division of the picture surface into related and balanced areas. For this reason, the theory of dynamic symmetry remains incomplete. Actually, lines and areas in a painting result from the space organization of the picture field. Space is the underlying structure of all painting. The art student must study space before he can satisfactorily get the effects he seeks.

There is no claim here for an exhaustive study of the various systems of pictorial space. Since one of the objectives here is to teach the reader to look at pictures intelligently, the theories of perspective are stated in an elementary way. They are described in action by analyses of representative examples from the great schools of art. This effort should thus act as a guide through the world of art. This survey of sources of the academic, naturalistic, abstract and non-objective painting should enable the reader to distinguish imitation from originality; and discriminate brilliant technical copying from genuine emotion and creative thinking.

CHAPTER ONE

Space

WHAT IS SPACE

The dictionary defines space as extension in all directions. That is sufficiently broad to encompass the efforts of thinkers, from Pythagoras to Einstein, who considered this extension in all directions objectively and tried to discover its laws, its limits and meaning. It is also inclusive to encompass the fears and fancies of primitive and pious minds who, in conceiving space subjectively, sought to explain and harness it with their faith. They populated the universe with personifications of their hopes and fears, and roamed its vastness in their imagination.

The artist is able to span both points of view. He can re-create the world as seen and understood objectively; or, he can interpret subjectively his own feelings and moods concerning it. The canvas, too, is space. Within itself it is infinite; and the painter is a creator in the picture-space universe. He defines its limits whether big, enclosing a vast landscape, or small, enclosing a still life. He can lead the beholder into the realm of the abstract, timeless and universal, or direct him to the concrete and temporal.

Throughout history, the artists explored the nature and possibilities of picture space just as the scientists explored the universe. They established systems of space organization which at all times were an expression of their knowledge of the world, and of their ideas concerning it. Here we will trace the evolution of the various systems concerned with the organization of space into the depth of the picture; and explain its function in modern art, where it has been immeasurably expanded by our increased scientific knowledge.

SPACE IN PAINTING

One of the basic problems of space organization is the distribution of forms, for the purpose of creating an illusion of recession into depth. Many theories have been evolved for its solution, each of them based on a particular concept of the function of art.

When the space of the canvas is considered, for instance, a hypothetical cube, its ground plane rises obliquely, enclosed by the other sides of the cube. In order to obtain the illusion of recession it is necessary here to overlap the forms along a diagonal line on a ground plane. There is necessarily no diminution of objects with distance. The cube is a geometrical concept which does not conform to optical law.

Diminution of objects as they move into depth is characteristic of perspective. The two basic systems of arrangement derived from this principle are, in historical sequence, one point perspective and two point perspective.

In one point perspective the canvas is seen frontally, like a stage; and the forms in space become smaller as they move into depth. Here all the recessive lines run obliquely from the four corners of the canvas, *converging* at a vanishing point in the center. The forms are symmetrically balanced on each side of a central axis which runs through the vanishing point.

When the frontal cube is turned and placed at an angle with the canvas, two point (angular) perspective is obtained. The picture may then be regarded as a window through which the stationary observer beholds an expanding vista. The obliquely *diverging* lines meet at vanishing points on each side of the picture. Paintings of this sort give an impression of expansion in space. The viewpoint here is the same as that of the camera, and conforms to optical law.

These basic systems of depicting three-dimensional space represent centuries of artistic evolution in Asia and Europe. They, together with their derivatives and variations, will be further discussed and illustrated in the subsequent chapters.

FLAT SPACE

The earliest attempts at portraying observable phenomena on a flat surface involved the representation of objects as they were known, and not as they appeared from a specific point of view. For instance, a square was always a square, regardless of the angle from which it was viewed, and was always drawn as a square. Representations of a cube were comparatively isometric. This approach to painting precluded the possibility of placing objects behind one another. It confined the artist to the two-dimensional surface of his picture.

Two-dimensional painting is characteristic of all primitive art, but when it continued to be used by growing civilizations it reached a high degree of perfection. This is most evident in the art of Egypt and Persia.

Primitive art began as a byproduct of religion. Early man populated the universe with superhuman creatures, or gods, to whom he ascribed all his fears and troubles. They were personifications of natural phenomena he could not control. To deal with them, he devised rituals designed to palliate their wrath and, if possible, to make them serve him. The magic of religious ceremony was for him an oasis of security. The primitive artist concerned himself with the recording of ideas. A herd of buffalos were so many individual buffalos. If he wanted to say that they were running, he painted their bodies in motion; and it is a testimony to his skill that our sophisticated eyes still see them moving with forcefulness. Moreover, they are moving not in relation to some fixed object, but in all space extended infinitely in all directions.

What produces this effect is the primitive artist's unawareness of natural law and optical principles. He could not conceive of enclosing a field of vision within the framework of his picture. He did not paint what his eyes saw, but what his mind perceived and found significant. His thinking was unscientific. He produced images floating unconditionally upon the two dimensional wall he was decorating.

The Egyptians showed a conceptual advance over the primitive by placing their forms and figures on a ground line. This was the earliest attempt at organizing space in painting. Their art was still confined to the two dimensional plane. The only way they indicated depth was by figures in front blotting out parts of those further back. All figures rest on the ground line and are primarily decorative.

Although their space device was primitive, their art was highly developed and enormously complex. They arranged their composition horizontally in symmetrically balanced areas, which reveal their mastery of rhythm and geometric design. Incidents are depicted by a series of figures and objects placed in sequence on the same wall, thereby indicating space and movement within a definite period of time. They present the life of Egypt in narrative form. Each figure contains a multiple view. The head is placed in profile, the eye is full. The shoulders and upper torso are also in full view, while the waist and lower limbs are again in profile. It is interesting to bear this in mind when we discuss modern painting in subsequent chapters.

The Greeks have contributed much to occidental culture, but as far as their painting is concerned we know practically nothing because no examples of it have come down to us. According to the writers of antiquity they had developed an elaborate system for representing space which influenced the Romans, examples of whose painting have been preserved in Pompeii. It is possible, however, that these writers referred to Graeco-Roman painting, which is far removed in time and style from the Greek classical period of the fifth century B. C.

The Greek vases of that period show little evidence of any system resembling or bordering on perspective. The designs are generally two-dimensional. The human figures are drawn true to life, revealing a highly developed technique of naturalistic representation. While designed on the flat plane, they might have been drawn from life. In battle scenes the figures are placed at different levels to suggest depth, but without diminution in size. Cubic objects such as chairs and chariots, are almost always presented in profile without any indication of volume.

Tradition has it that Roman painting is derived from the Greek. Roman murals have been discovered in Rome, Pompeii and other places near Mt. Vesuvius where they were buried by volcanic ash in 79 A.D. They show that the Roman artists, of the Empire, had advanced beyond the flat surface and were trying to portray three-dimensional space. For the first time in the history of art we find figures placed on a ground plane, receding into depth. This is a long way from the two-dimensional ground line of the Egyptians.

In rendering large volumes of space, such as rooms or buildings, the Romans came very near to perspective; but they lacked a unifying principle and therefore their lines do not converge properly. It is interesting to note that this art closely resembles late medieval painting.

A clearly defined system for portraying a volume of space appears first in Oriental art in the Persian print (Plate III). It is demonstrated by the diagonal walls which enclose the room. But the Persians were faced with an insoluble problem when they tried to portray the tile decorations on the floor. They knew, of course, the metrical design of the pattern but were ignorant of any means by which it could be transferred to the picture surface with the proper foreshortening. Instead, they created a flat design which is perfect in itself.

CHAPTER TWO

First Attempts Into Space

THE THREE TIERS AND THE CUBE OF THE CANVAS

Attempts at freeing forms from the flat surface of the picture, and giving them the appearance of existing in space, gradually evolved into the first principle of space design which will be studied in the Byzantine "Transfiguration of Christ."

The "Transfiguration of Christ" (Plate II) employs the most primitive device for portraying space before the discovery of the cube. Here the picture was divided into three planes (Fig. I). The lowest plane is the nearest, and recession is obtained by placing one plane above the other on the picture surface. The upper three figures (the two saints and Christ), despite the fact that they are larger than those in front, appear set back in space. Scale and size are determined by symbolic importance in complete disregard of the rules of perspective. This is also demonstrated by the trees, which are squeezed down to fit into the design. The natural scale is completely ignored. To the Medievalist, nature served merely as a background for the spiritual struggle of man. His art expresses his total absorption with spiritual values.

Mystic art, of this kind, is constructed vertically on the picture plane. It ignores the horizontal (the earth) and aspires upward, to the heavens. It reaches into that rarified realm of unbounded space where the mind contemplates eternity and treats forms abstractly, as symbols of the spirit.

PLATE II

Courtesy of The Detroit Institute of Arts

PLATE II. THE TRANSFIGURATION. BYZANTINE CLOISONNE (12th Century)

The symbolism of this cloisonné bears analysis. Its very division into three planes is the result of a metaphysical interpretation of life. The ground plane represents the earth; the middle, an intervening realm between the earth and Heaven; and the uppermost plane, Heaven itself. On the ground plane are three mortals struggling in the toils of earthly imperfection.

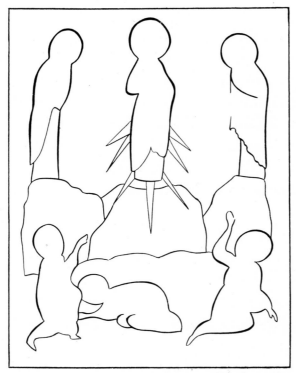

Figure 1. The Three Tiers

Two saints stand on the mountaintops. They symbolize the highest level between man and God. On top is the central figure, the highest peak, God. He is framed by as perfect a symbol of the universe as can be found in all art; the circles, defining the motion of the worlds around Him, and the stars studding the blue universe in formal array. Seven flames issue

23

from His figure, possibly symbolizing the cabalistic concept of the seven emanations of God. Inlays of red, blue, green and yellow, play beautifully against a gold background, which stands for the spirituality of life. The picture is non-real, abstract, a pictorial interpretation of Catholic theology.

The layout of this picture is symmetrical (evenly balanced on both sides of a central axis). It contains a fundamental order of composition found in many pre-Renaissance and Renaissance paintings. For instance, Giotto and Michelangelo used this kind of composition in their pictures "The Last Judgment." It served as a layout for many of El Greco's paintings. In Raphael's "Transfiguration" and "School of Athens" the same basic arrangement was utilized. However, the Byzantine "Transfiguration of Christ" is composed vertically, the scale being guided by design and symbolic importance, while Raphael's fresco is constructed horizontally, rigidly adhering to the rule of perspective. This contrast shows the wide rift that finally occurred between Medieval and Renaissance Art.

THE CUBE OF THE CANVAS

The principle of the cube was the earliest known method for obtaining an illusion of space in painting. It was the foundation of Oriental and pre-Renaissance art and expressed the space awareness of people whose knowledge of physical law was limited and whose concept of art was conditioned by a philosophy which was speculative rather than scientific. In contrast to perspective, which is derived from optical principles, the cube belongs to the realm of pictorial design. While both systems have much in common, we shall see that they worked toward divergent ends.

The lack of an optical principle did not in the least impair the artistic creativeness of the Orientals. On the contrary, their creative efforts, unhindered by the necessity of imitating reality, were free to fashion works of art in which emphasis could be laid upon design, inherent quality and expression, rather than photographic similarity. To appreciate their achievements we must dismiss the yardstick of Renaissance standards.

The cube is a key to these early art forms, since it conditioned the type of design and space organization that characterizes Oriental painting, and made for qualities which are unique in the history of art.

THE THEORY OF THE CUBE

When the space of the canvas is considered a hypothetical cube, this cube functions as the basis for a definite system of pictorial

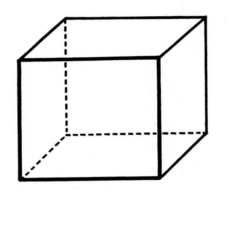

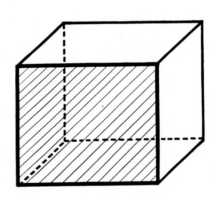

Figure 2. The Hypothetical Cube

Figure 3. The Picture Plane

space. It is primarily a method for obtaining the recession of forms into the depth of the picture.

The cube may be described as an "arena" within which forms are placed to represent a landscape, a still life, a portrait, an abstraction, or any other subject.

The cube is by no means ordinary. The following are its characteristics;

(a) It is *always* looked into *from above* and *one side* (Fig. 2). This is necessary to make the ground plane appear diagonal;

(b) *It has no definite size,* and the artist may use it in any way he desires; it may be rectangular or square, deep or shallow, as will be demonstrated in subsequent analyses of paintings;

(c) It is the "arena" within which the actors (lines, planes and volumes) perform their choreography according to the artist's bidding.

THE PICTURE PLANE

The only tangible element of the cube is its front plane (Fig. 3), which is actually the picture surface (the canvas on which the artist is working). This is called the *picture plane.* The picture plane serves the following purposes:

(a) It is the first dimension from which all forms recede into space;

(b) It is the surface upon which all forms are recorded for the purpose of decoration or spacial illusion;

(c) It is an area limited by two vertical and two horizontal borders;

(d) Vertically, when discussed in relation to the movements of planes within the cube, it is referred to as the vertical plane of the canvas; It is interesting to note that metaphysical art is usually constructed vertically, parallel to the picture surface;

(e) A picture is decorative when the forms are designed flat upon the picture plane.

THE GROUND PLANE

True metaphysical art expresses itself abstractly. It builds vertically, parallel to the picture plane. It tends toward symbolic decoration. As the thoughts of man turned from religion

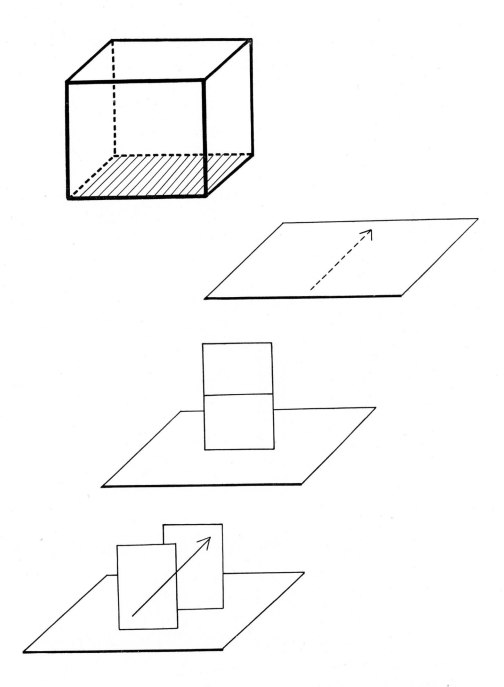

Figure 4. The Ground Plane

Figure 5. The Recessive Diagonal

Figure 6. Plane on Plane

Figure 7. Overlapping Planes

27

toward naturalism, he extended his technique to meet the new requirements and began to use the ground plane of the cube (Fig. 4). This is well demonstrated in the transition from early Byzantine art to the naturalism of the Renaissance.

The ground plane functions as follows:

(a) It is the plane on which the forms are placed so as to obtain a horizontal movement into depth;

(b) The nearest line of the ground plane is the bottom border of the picture plane. From it, the ground plane move backward into space. This near border therefore is the *first* tangible dimension of the picture.

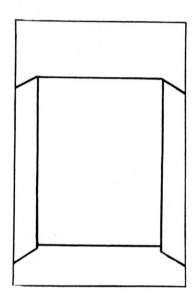

Figure 8. The First Cube

THE DIAGONAL OF RECESSION AND OVERLAPPING PLANES

The cube of the canvas is the hypothesis from which the principle of recession is derived.

(a) Due to the fact that the cube is viewed obliquely from above, a line as it moves back into space on the ground plane rises diagonally as it recedes (Fig. 5);

(b) If one plane is placed directly above another plane, it is difficult to decide if the upper plane is on top or behind the lower one (Fig. 6);

(c) However, if the two planes are placed diagonally against each other, then the upper plane appears back in space relative to the lower one. Therefore, to obtain a movement into depth planes must be placed diagonally (Fig. 7). This assures their positive relationship in space. The diagonal line of movement between planes is called the *diagonal of recession*.

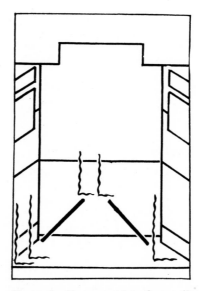

Figure 9. Movement into Space (Persian)

The principles of the overlapping plane and the recessive diagonal, derived from the cube, are among the fundamental devices which create the effect of forms receding into the depth of the canvas. They are not only characteristic of early painting but may be found as late as Vermeer. Contemporary abstractions again employ them to create space.

THE FIRST CUBE
The 16th Century Persian print "Marriage of King Khusrau and Shirin" (Plate III) shows an elementary application

of the cube principle. Its composition, while constructed vertically of evenly balanced squares and rectangles, still im-

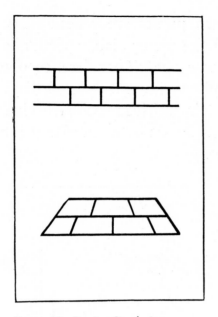

Figure 10. Persian Rendering

Figure 10a. Perspective Rendering

plies a volume of space outlined by the diagonal walls on each side of the room (Fig. 8). This enclosure is adequately obtained without interfering with the decoration or the beautiful ornamented surface. The three basic line movements, the horizontal, the vertical and the diagonal are here utilized in all their purity. Distance has been implied by a diagonal from the near figures to the lovers on the dais (Fig. 9), while the back wall stays behind the two columns. This penetration into space is instantly negated by the formalized ornamentations which vibrate on the picture surface like sparkling jewels.

The Persians had developed a system of foreshortening only as it pertained to large areas, like the side walls of the room. However, as previously stated, they had no means of foreshortening the tiles on the floor (Fig. 10) in their true geometric relationship (Fig. 10a). It must be emphasized that this

PLATE III

Courtesy of The Metropolitan Museum of Art

PLATE III. MARRIAGE OF KING KHUSRAU AND SHIRIN. PERSIAN (16th Century)

is a qualitative, rather than a negative, observation. The Persians, within their area of awareness, created art of rare distinction.

In this print space is approached frontally. All diagonal planes recede to a perpendicular axis in the middle of the picture. This makes for a symmetrical composition, equal forms balancing each other on both sides of the center. Compositions of this kind may be found throughout the early Renaissance. Similar form arrangements resulting, on the one hand, from an elementary cube priniciple and, on the other, from an elementary awareness of perspective, offer insight into the kind of mental qualities which conditioned early painting. The primitive space principle of the Renaissance, for instance, was merely the start on the scientific road which finally led to modern art. The Persians, on the contrary, seemed perfectly content with their system. Within its framework they created an integrated art, complete within itself and thoroughly suited to a culture which regarded painting primarily as decoration. In both cases, the frontal approach was the door which led into pictorial space.

This picture contains the type of symmetrical design and geometric pattern characteristic of Persian art. It has rich and splendid colors, opulent and varied ornament. Design patterns of unexcelled craftsmanship animate the whole surface. Formal design, rhythmic line (note figures in Plate III), jewel-like color and texture (observe the tiles in the foreground in contrast to the robes of the figures and the rug on the dais) combine contrapuntally for harmony and beauty. If one loves quality this picture is a feast for the eyes. It must be minutely examined, and sensuously enjoyed, as it was no doubt examined and enjoyed by the luxuriant 16th century Oriental court for whose dilection it was created.

33

OVERLAPPING PLANES AND THE RECESSIVE DIAGONAL

The Chinese painting, "Landscape" (Plate IV), demonstrates the application of the principle of the overlapping planes and the recessive diagonal in its simplest form (Fig. 11). The nearest plane in the picture is the water, from which a *line* zig-zags upward, following the path of a *receding diagonal* along the course of the waterfall. From there it moves to the first and second mountain top and to the darkened sun *in overlapping planes*. The mist in the center of the picture also recedes diagonally from near to far, parallel with the plane of the water at the bottom. These lines of recession define the placement of the forms in space. They are not only the *unifying structure* which locks the forms in place, but also outline the paths the eyes must follow.

Within this space pattern the mountains are superbly nuanced in tone value, the contour lines are most sensitively accented, and only those qualities are selected from nature which lend themselves to aesthetic considerations. The Orientals would consider the inclusion of detail for the sake of realism in bad taste. The key to Chinese taste may be found in their caligraphy, where not only the quality of the stroke is most carefully considered, but also the relationship of the lines to each other. This emphasis on the rhythmic stroke, the interplay of tone and line, was established early in Chinese civilization, and remained pure until it was corrupted by European influence.

Nature plays an important role in Oriental art. The beauties of the countryside, vast mountain ranges, enveloping mists and waterfalls are revealed with poetic vision as a world of fantasy. It is an art which expresses love for the joys of life. It is always in exquisite taste; and the moods of nature, mysticism, folklore and myth are interpreted in rhythmic terms as in a song.

PLATE IV

PLATE IV. CHINESE LANDSCAPE

From the Renaissance to the late 19th century Oriental painting was misunderstood in the West mainly because its system of design was not derived from theories of perspective which were considered fundamental to any good painting. The average connoisseur, therefore, regarded it as the expression of

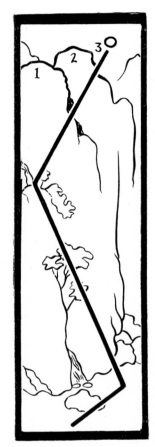

Figure 11. The Receding Diagonal (Chinese)

a foreign people whose art was primitive and barbaric. Oriental painting had to await the advent of Impressionism for a true evaluation of its merits. The impressionists, in their efforts to free themselves from the bondage of the Renaissance, were the first to seek inspiration and guidance in cultures outside Europe. They started the trend which also led to the revival of interest in primitive and prehistoric art forms.

THE COMPLETED ENCLOSURE.

The 18th century Japanese print (Plate V) contains the kind of design which results from a mastery of the cube principle. The picture contains only a part of the room (Fig. 12),

Figure 12. The Oblique Cube (Japanese)

and yet, a complete enclosure has been obtained by a sweeping line of movement which starts from the nearest figure, moves back with the figures into depth, follows the back walls, and then returns to the starting point (Fig. 13). Recession is satisfactorily obtained despite the fact that there is no convergence to vanishing points, as in perspective. Note that the three figures are placed one behind the other, in accordance with the principle of overlapping planes (Fig. 14).

In contrast to the more primitive frontal and horizontal arrangement of the Persian print, the space in this picture is viewed *obliquely,* every plane moving diagonally into depth.

This is a very mature approach. Its results have much in common with the space composition of the 16th century European painting, employed extensively by Brueghel and Vermeer. The parallel development of the elementary cube into the per-

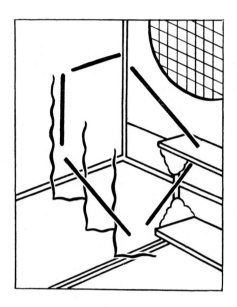

Figure 13. The Completed Enclosure (Japanese)

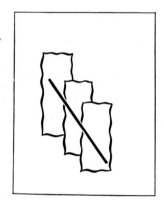

Figure 14. Overlapping Planes (Japanese)

spective space of the West, on the one hand, and the completed cube as found in this print, on the other, both attaining an equivalent oblique space arrangement under different systems, indicates that the lack of perspective in Japanese art may not have been due to ignorance but to other considerations. The decorative element, for instance, plays an important part in this picture. The planes, while moving diagonally in space, are still so shaped as to form *related geometric patterns* on the picture surface. The cube offers a system for plastic suggestion in depth, while at the same time allowing sufficient latitude for the artist to adjust planes, lines and tones for aesthetic purposes.

PLATE V

Courtesy of The Metropolitan Museum of Art

PLATE V. JAPANESE PRINT (18th Century) HARUNOBU, SUZUKI

CHAPTER THREE

Medieval Painting

SPACE IN MEDIEVAL PAINTING

Medieval painting may be considered semi-Oriental. It has its roots in Coptic and Middle Eastern art, and is the result of the merging of East and West. The Oriental cube was extended and ramified as art slowly made its way towards the perspective painting of the Renaissance. With Giotto the Renaissance cube finally took shape. For the first time objects were foreshortened in perspective which, however, had to await Alberti for scientific definition.

The search for a new space principle is found throughout Medieval painting, and is the cause of the continual reshuffling of planes. Diverse attempts at perspective are prevalent. At times planes are jumbled about in the picture, and sides of buildings are precariously placed in space. In emulation of the sculptor, the Medieval painter attempted to create forms in the third dimension. He wanted to describe them in space. The picture no longer dealt with purely decorative illusion. It attempted reality, the portrayal of dimension containing weight and volume.

Religion furnished the subject matter for Medieval painting. Life was interpreted in terms of the scriptures. The Medieval mind was religious, metaphysical. The artist's exploration of space was the germ which gradually destroyed his world, and paved the way for the scientific age of the Renaissance.

44

"The Birth of St. John the Baptist" by Paolo Veneziano (Plate VI) is a typical example of pre-Renaissance space design. Its box-like structure demonstrates that the Medievalist reverted to fundamentals in his efforts to establish a solid foundation for new departures into space.

What has happened here to the cube is worthy of examination. It is presented obliquely, according to the rules, but here the artist tried to converge diagonal planes, aiming at perspective. This is the dawn of a new space consciousness.

Figure 15. The Medieval Cube

In this picture the subject is set back from the picture plane, the monk on the left being the nearest form from which the cube recedes into space. This solid construction of the cube is something new in European art (Fig. 15). At times it appeared inside the picture, removed from the picture plane, the other forms being ranged around it in unlimited space. These unorthodox variations of the cube are attempts at a new theory for the placement of forms in space.

In this respect, the Medievalists act as a link between the Oriental cube theory and the era of perspective inaugurated by Giotto. And yet, it is noteworthy to observe in this picture how satisfactorily the small table at the monk's feet goes back into space, despite the fact that it refutes the perspective theory of convergence. The picture transcends time by presenting the story on several planes simultaneously: the monk in front, the main drama in the center of the box, and the gossips in the door at the right. This inclusion of all the pertinent facts of the story carries the picture beyond the range of the camera, which circumscribed later pictures. This most primitive manifestation of the transcendence of time finds a sympathetic parallel in the time-space interpretations of modern painting.

In 1308, the painter Duccio (1260?-1319?) was commissioned by the town council of Siena to paint a series of panels depicting the life of Christ. In 1311 he completed the "Maesta" with the enthusiastic approval of his patrons. A holiday was declared in his honor and the masterpiece was carried in triumph to the cathedral. Many of the panels have since been dispersed among museums throughout the world. Three are in this country, and the "Temptation of Christ" (Plate VII) hangs in the Frick Collection in New York.

The composition of this picture is masterfully mature. While retaining qualities derived from the Byzantine (vertical construction in infinite space), it still reaches into the third dimension. Its form placement and linear movement anticipate many masterpieces of a later date. We have seen that the divergence of diagonal line movements from a near point back into space was fundamental to the construction of the Japanese print. It will also be found basic to the paintings of the 17th century.

The line movements which enclose the whole picture are derived from the cube. Within this framework lines radiate in a whirling spiral from the central figures, Christ and Satan (Fig. 16). The movement from the central forms to the out-lying ones has the effect of a view seen through a curved, sharp

Figure 16. Movements in Space (Duccio)

angle lens. The forms, as they near the borders of the picture, twist into a circular movement in order to remain in focus, which is centered on the main figure. Every form in the picture is designed to move rhythmically within a single pattern.

Abstractly, the picture is composed as a design in which every line and form is integrated into a harmonious and con-tinuously interlocking unit. In this sense this picture exempli-fies distortion in art—where natural forms are deliberately shaped into the design demanded by subjective necessity.

In contrast to the two-dimensional character of Byzantine art, this picture is composed in three dimensional volumes, each receding according to the principle of the cube (Fig. 16).

Their arrangement anticipates the spacial expansion which took place in the 17th century. The solid forms, representing earthly existence, again give evidence of the transition to the naturalism of the Renaissance.

A great change has also occurred in the subject matter of the paintings. The "Transfiguration of Christ" symbolizes the doctrine of Catholicism, whereas "The Temptation of Christ" deals with the moral struggle of man: the battle, and the triumph of good over evil. It states that, in the spiritual life, the righteous are rewarded with eternal peace, while all the horrors of hell, so weirdly implied by the figure of Satan, are predicted for the transgressor. Imagine with what reverence—and fear—Duccio's contemporaries contemplated this picture. How, as they stood before it, they felt that they were viewing the titanic struggle of spiritual forces of which they were an integral part; that their lives were inevitably woven into the pattern of moral struggle which, according to their earthly conduct, rewarded them with a future existence of eternal bliss, or condemned them to unspeakable torture.

Nature played a subordinate part in this drama. It was merely man's temporal abode. For him there was no reality beyond that described in the Scriptures, and nature appeared inorganic and lifeless.

PLATE VII

Courtesy of The Frick Collection

PLATE VII. THE TEMPTATION OF CHRIST. DUCCIO

CHAPTER FOUR

Perspective

THE OPTICAL PRINCIPLE

The discovery of perspective marks the dawn of the era of enlightenment when western man turned from theology to the study of natural law for the verification of facts. The artist, reflecting this trend, found in science a new world of ideas which he instantly adopted for aesthetic purposes. He not only became conscious of the problem of optical space and searched through mathematics for its formula, but also became an anatomist and dissected the human body in order to understand its mechanisms. This pattern of naturalistic investigation, begun during the Renaissance, stamped the attitude of the artist toward art for generations to come.

The trend toward realism is evident in the art of the late 14th and early 15th centuries when all the artists endeavored to master the problem of foreshortening the cube in perspective. This optical awareness may be defined as factual-visual. The artist, while conscious of the geometrical (sculptured) proportions of the object, had learned to portray it on a flat surface, as it would appear to the eye of the stationary beholder.

The man who accomplished this feat was the architect Leon Battista Alberti (1404-1472) who between 1435-1436 discovered the formula of three dimensional perspective by constructing his famous box, the floor of which was a checkerboard (Fig. 17). It was a mathematical formula for the foreshortening of checkerboard squares (the ground plane) on a flat surface (the picture plane) as they *appear* in related depths — that is, visualized in space according to a geometric system. This theory of one point perspective, also called parallel perspective, was used by all the Renaissance artists as the underlying structure for their spacial composition.

To avoid repetition of that which has already been sufficiently covered in other works, only the most elementary facts, which are necessary for an understanding of the perspective theory, will be treated here.

In the following pages we will consider the development of space construction from the 14th century to the high Renaissance (from Giotto to Raphael). In the beginning the artists constructed a cubic box much like a stage set, into which they placed their forms. Gradually they acquired more freedom, and at the height of the Renaissance employed one-point perspective in all its ramifications.

Figure 17. Alberti's Perspective Box
(after W. M. Ivins Jr., "Rationalization of Sight")

An example of the enthusiasm with which the early Renaissance artists adopted the theory of perspective may be found in the story of Ucello, who is said to have lain awake nights marveling at the beauties of this newly discovered science. To these painters perspective was the ultimate in the expression of reality. The space procedure initiated by Giotto

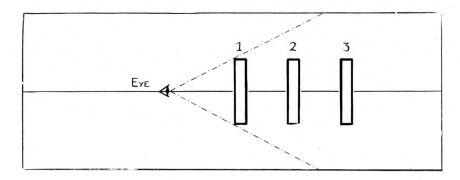

Figure 18. Expanding Vision

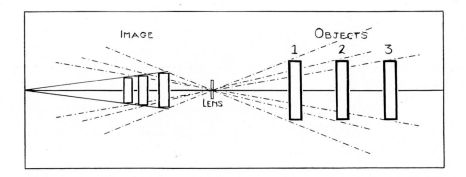

Figure 19. Apparent Shrinkage of Objects

was employed without basic divergence by the great painters throughout the Renaissance.

THE APPARENT SHRINKAGE OF OBJECTS

The dictionary defines perspective as pertaining to the science of optics. Perspective attempts to portray the related appearance of objects as they may be traced on a flat surface (the picture plane) from the viewpoint of the stationary observer. The reasons for this apparent distortion of objects, namely, their shrinkage as they recede into distance toward a point on the horizon, are explained in figures 18 and 19.

In figure 18, the lines of vision expand outward from the eye of the observer into space. The poles "1," "2," "3" occupy equal distances from each other in space. However, relative to the eye, pole "1" occupies the full area of vision, while "2" and "3" appear proportionately smaller. The distant poles decrease, in apparent size, in proportion to the increase of the field of vision.

In figure 19, a further ramification of the same phenomenon is explained by the use of a camera as follows: The lens (like the eye) receives light waves from the outside, and projects them as images on a receptive film equivalent to the retina. Lines of sight from poles "1," "2" and "3" radiate from the objects to the lens, creating angles relative in degree to their distance from the camera. This results in the size of the object as it appears on the film. Notice the apparent size of "2" and "3" on the "1" pole.

This is a simple demonstration of the physical process of sight; and yet, there is much more to it than that. A marvelous process of readjustment takes place before the images, received on the retina, are reconstructed mentally with a full realization of their placement and proportions. The capacity to recognize is in the realm of psychology and will be studied in Chapter Eight.

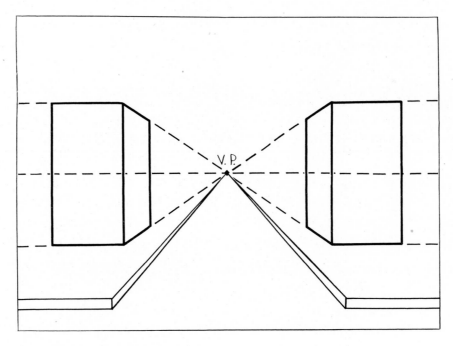

Figure 20. One Point Perspective

ONE POINT PERSPECTIVE

In one point perspective (Fig. 20) there is but one vanishing point (v.p.) in the center of the picture. The side planes of the box converge to meet at this central point on the horizon (eye-level). The front planes, however, remain frontal and parallel and *do not converge* — for which reason this system is also called parallel perspective. One point perspective is a *fundamental principle*, the *first law of optics*.

CHAPTER FIVE

Renaissance Perspective

THE MAN OF THE RENAISSANCE

When Western man turned away from metaphysics and began asking questions about nature, he had to rediscover methods of objective scientific inquiry. As the pure faith of the Medievalist gave way to scepticism, he demanded empirical proof for the categorical statements of theology.

The conflict between science and religion split the personality of the man of the Renaissance. His rational necessity for proof clashed with a deeply inherited need for an unquestioning religion, causing an irreconcilable ambivalence to which may be attributed much that is contradictory in Renaissance art.

Religion supplied the subject matter for Renaissance painting. But now it served merely as a facade behind which the painter indulged his real love for nature, humanity, physical beauty, and the problem of form in space. He became conscious of the landscape, and painted his religious theme into the familiar environment of the local scene. He painted his loved one — his ideal — in the guise of the madonna. With the loss of subjective conviction he became interested in technical perfection, the rendering of draperies and materials, the problems of modeled forms, chiaroscuro, and the mastery of perspective. In the dark brooding of Michelangelo's titanic art and the enigmatic implications of Leonardo da Vinci's Madonnas, with their deep backgrounds of mysterious landscapes,

PLATE VIII

PLATE VIII. THE MOCKING OF CHRIST. GIOTTO
ARENA CHAPEL, PADUA

may be found the courageous Renaissance man, daring to venture into the forbidden territory of his own passions and speculations.

THE RENAISSANCE BOX

The space and the substance of Renaissance art became first evident in the work of the pioneering genius, Giotto (1226-1337).

In "The Mocking of Christ" (Plate VIII) the space is definitely shaped as an enclosure, extended by receding walls which

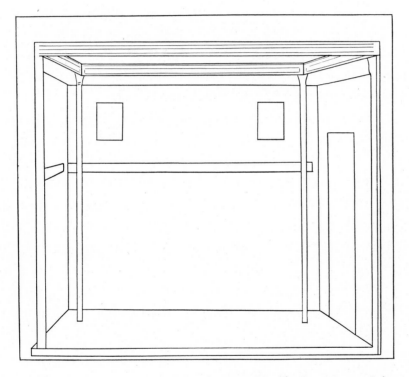

Figure 21. The Renaissance Cube

reveal an awareness of one point perspective (Fig. 21). It is apparent that the artist was conscious of the optics of convergence but, presumably, did not know its mathematical formula.

63

To better understand as to what has happened, it may be well to contrast Giotto's space with that of the Medievalists. The cube has now been extended into a perspective volume enclosing three dimensional space forms. Giotto's cube is the key to the space of the Renaissance.

In the art of Giotto humanistic interest found its first concrete manifestations. Giotto studied man, the individual; he watched him in his gestures and emotional outbursts and he became conscious of three dimensional form in space. In contrast to the Byzantines, who preached theology, and Duccio, who preached morality, Giotto's art dealt with the drama of the religious human being.

In "The Death of St. Francis" (Plate IX), Giotto constructed his box of space like a stage set (Fig. 22) into which he placed the figures for dramatic presentation. He composed his picture as a pantomime. Like a choreographer, he organized his "actors" for maximum dramatic effect.

This fresco is heroic in its dramatic simplicity, perfect in its composition and motivated by one profound emotion: the death of St. Francis. Gestures of anxiety, grief, reverence, love and prayer express the essence of human emotion. They demonstrate a fundamental quality of creative genius, to animate a form as if it were impelled by an inner force, a living emotion. The picture, while profound in its human understanding, still retains the medieval viewpoint in its genuine religious fervor. It expresses the spirit of the early Renaissance, and reveals Giotto as the great genius of his time and as one of the giants in art.

SPACE IN MID-RENAISSANCE

The Renaissance was a cultural movement to which all artists contributed and to which all conformed. Certain conventions were universally accepted. The artist strove to excel in the established mode. Each formed a link and contributed his creative energies to complete the line of continuous growth

PLATE IX

PLATE IX.   THE DEATH OF ST. FRANCIS.   GIOTTO
CHURCH OF SANTA CROCE, FLORENCE

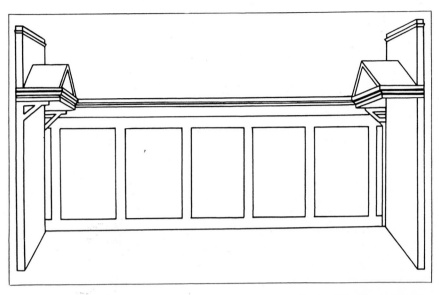

Figure 22. The Stage Box

from Duccio and Giotto to Raphael and Michelangelo. History tends to distort fact by isolating the artist from his age and attributing to his genius conventions which had already been established by tradition. The Renaissance artist did not exist in a creative vacuum. Any study of Renaissance painting shows how dependent the artists were upon each other, how freely they borrowed from one another and bodily took from their predecessors and contemporaries anything that suited their own ends. Great art can flourish only in a soil of this kind, where genius is not an isolated individual, but the most perfect expression of the age.

Masaccio (1401-1428) takes his place in history as the man who initiated the "grand style" of the High Renaissance. His fresco "St. Peter Resuscitating The Son of The King of Antioch" (Plate X) was left incomplete, for Masaccio died at the early age of twenty-eight. He painted the central group of figures. The kneeling boy and the outlying groups were added some sixty years later by Filippino Lippi. Masaccio's dependence on the space structure of Giotto is quite evident. However, the evolution of the high Renaissance is revealed in the

67

penetration of space beyond the back wall, in this case showing the trees in the garden. Besides, the boxed room has been replaced by a courtyard, the tendency being to enlarge the enclosed space (Fig. 23).

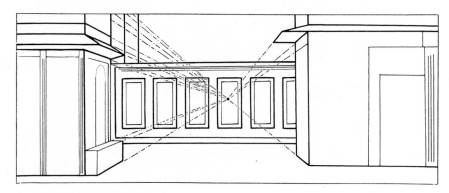

Figure 23. The Enlarged Stage

Variations on the type of composition exemplified by this fresco may be found throughout the art of this period. It demonstrates the transition of pictorial space in the ever expanding Renaissance. Not only did Masaccio learn from his predecessors, but the Brancacci Chapel, which contains his work (of which this fresco is a part), served Raphael and Michelangelo as a source of inspiration in their early years.

RENAISSANCE PERSPECTIVE

"The Last Supper" was a common theme in Renaissance art. Among the great painters who rendered it were Andrea del Castagno (in 1450), Ghirlandajo (in 1480) Andrea del Sarto (in 1527), and Leonardo da Vinci (1452-1519). The similarity of presentation in all these frescoes is startling. Leonardo da Vinci's masterpiece (Plate XI) differs from the rest not in form but in genius. The coincidence between his space structure and the previous examples is evident. It is as

PLATE X

if a stage set in simple perspective had been established early in the Renaissance, and the artists throughout the period rearranged the props and furnishings according to the play to be performed.

In this composition the table is placed close to the picture plane. The drama takes place behind it, giving us the impression that we are spectators viewing a performance. Space is created within the framework of one point perspective. All receding planes converge to a central vanishing point behind the head of Christ, and every perspective line points to, or

Figure 24. Renaissance Perspective

radiates from Him, the central figure (Fig. 24). The composition is symmetrical, balanced on each side of a central axis, which is the type of arrangement resulting from one point perspective. Within this symmetrical space the figures behind the table are superbly organized in pantomime, in groups of three. Note the use of Alberti's checkerboard in the foreshortened squares on the ceiling. The balanced relationships of all the planes, derived by mathematical formula, result in a universally harmonious space, revealing the intention of the Renaissance mind to find a key to the mystery of nature in science. Leonardo sought beauty, not through intuition, but through order. Within the magical formula of three dimensional space he recreated the drama of humanity not simply like Giotto, who synthesized the essence of human emotion through gesture, but in the grand manner of the high Renaissance. The figures were all stylized, heroic; the presentation, a dramatic world—populated by human beings—whose dignity, stature and grand demeanor reflect the Renaissance mentality and aspirations.

"The School of Athens" (Plate XII) by Raphael (1483-1520) represents the fruition of Renaissance objectives. The possibilities of Renaissance space were almost exhausted. Despite elaborate complications of ornament and architecture, it is apparent how carefully Raphael constructed his space on the principle of one point perspective. There is no guesswork here. The construction is mathematical; the stage set is built according to rule, with the foreshortened squares on the front plane of the floor again derived from Alberti's checkerboard. The use of convention by no means detracts from the greatness of this fresco. On the contrary, the sheer invention of architectural forms, constructed within a predetermined space, makes this a work of rare distinction. It is a summation of all the knowledge which the artists of that day had attained in their efforts to express the mystery of natural law through art.

It must be understood that a performance of this kind was not the work of one man alone. Raphael, as contractor, was in a position to employ the best available minds as his assistants. His uncle, for instance, was architect to the pope. He also had a tradition of three hundred years upon which to draw. This work may be said to have absorbed all the technical knowledge which the Renaissance had to offer, under the guidance of one of its leading minds—Raphael.

PLATE XI

PLATE XI. THE LAST SUPPER.   LEONARDO DA VINCI
MONASTERY OF S. MARIA DELLA GRAZIE, MILAN

PLATE XII

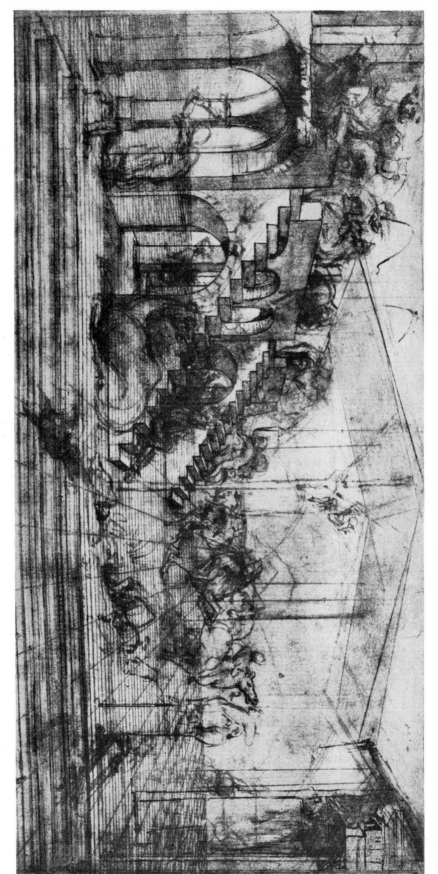

PLATE XIII

PLATE XIII. PERSPECTIVE DRAWING. LEONARDO DA VINCI

PLATE XIV

Courtesy of The Metropolitan Museum of Art

PLATE XIV. THE SET FOR COMEDIES
FROM SERLINO "LE SECOND LIVRE DE PERSPECTIVE", PARIS, 1545

CHAPTER SIX

Angular Perspective

PERSPECTIVE IN THE 16TH AND 17TH CENTURIES

Attempts to place buildings obliquely within a frontal cube arrangement may be found as early as the 14th and 15th centuries in isolated works of Giotto, Taddeo Gaddi, Fra Angelico and others. This happened rarely and it emphasized, by contrast, the uniform pattern to which all the artists of the Renaissance conformed. These early attempts at oblique foreshortening were far ahead of their times. Obviously, they were too advanced and had to await the solution of elementary perspective problems before they could become the serious concern of the artist and mathematician. Presumably, for this reason, the artists persisted in their conventionally established space pattern (one point perspective) exploring all possibilities of this first principle.

During the 16th century angular perspective first emerged as a method of space organization. How and when the artists became aware of the important fact that when a cube is viewed obliquely each side has its own set of vanishing lines, receding to the horizon, history does not make clear. The theory was supplied by Vignold, Guidobaldo del Monte and others, who had done much research in this area. Its application to painting appears first in the work of the Baroque painters, the Spaniards and the Dutch.

Angular perspective instantly dated the Renaissance prin-

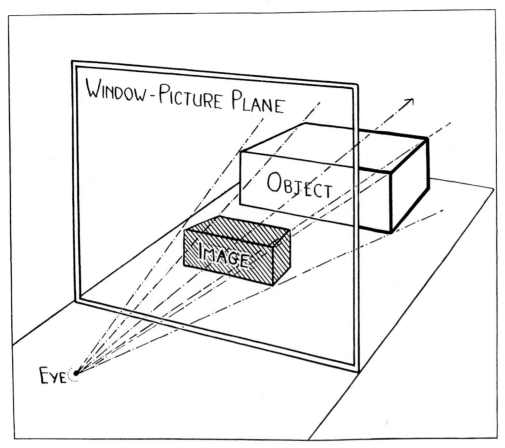

Figure 25. Image on Window

ciple as elementary geometry. In its multiple applications, it furnished a formula by which the visual field of the picture could be infinitely extended and nature more truthfully represented. It opened a new world of pictorial space for the artist to explore.

Angular perspective brought the picture into the realm of camera vision; it furnished a closer approach to optical reality than any system of the past.

THE PRINCIPLE OF ANGULAR PERSPECTIVE

The outline of a box traced on a window pane is a reproduction of the box in angular perspective (Fig. 25).

Figure 26 defines the elementary principle of angular perspective. In this drawing objects are viewed obliquely, turned to one side, which results in a convergence of all the lines, each to its own vanishing point (v.p.). These vanishing points are always on the horizon, which is a horizontal line at eye level.

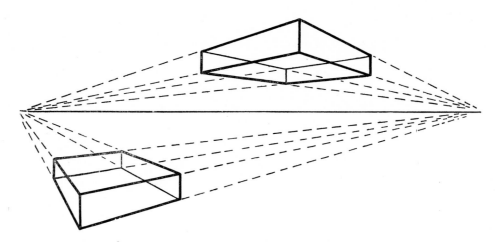

Figure 26. Angular Perspective

ANGULAR PERSPECTIVE-APPLICATION

The "Wedding Feast" (Plate XV) by Peter Brueghel (1525-1569) is an excellent example of the new space theories developed in the 16th century. A comparison of this painting with any of the Renaissance reveals the enormous progress made. Space was approached obliquely instead of frontally. In contrast to the simple perspective of the Renaissance, Brueghel's painting contained a multiple perspective picture world.

Angular perspective offered the artist of the 16th century the means with which to express the new attitudes, resulting from social evolution and religious reformation. It gave him a

84

PLATE XV

PLATE XV. WEDDING FEAST. PETER BRUEGHEL
VIENNA, MUSEUM

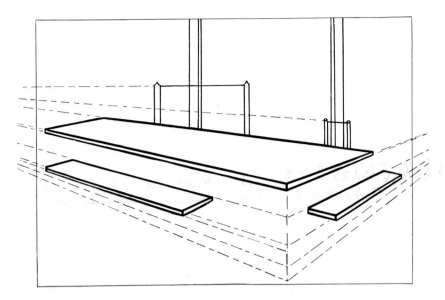

Figure 27. Sixteenth Century Space

new point of view and opened wider and ever expanding vistas. The formula of optical mechanics had been finally discovered. The stage presentations of Giotto, composed in pantomime, disappeared completely. The picture now functioned as a window revealing life in all its different humors.

The discovery of angular perspective brought about a vital change in the spacial arrangement of the picture (Fig. 27). It threw the symmetrical design of the Renaissance completely off balance. The artist could no longer compose equally on each side of a central axis. The primary weight of his composition. shifted to one side, required a balance of unequal parts, resulting in a new kind of organization.

The symmetrical box of the Renaissance, with its *contraction* of space, demanded that the main action take place in front, close to the picture plane (Fig. 28). In angular perspective space expanded with distance and the main action was set back, being related to a few large forms in front (Fig. 29). This

87

Figure 28. Contraction

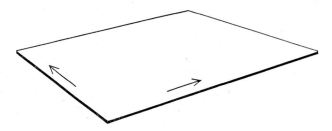

Figure 29. Expansion

oblique approach greatly elaborated the elementary Renaissance geometry of perspective. It set the pattern for composition in painting up to Cezanne, who again jolted the space world of the picture, reshuffling the planes into a new order.

"The Wedding Feast" also demonstrates the humanistic outlook, which was another great difference between Brueghel and Giotto. Unlike Giotto, Brueghel, in the main, eliminated religion from his text. Religion had lost now some of its influence and was no longer the focal point of intellectual activity. It ceased to be the main source of inspiration for the creative artist, who expresses for his age that which is most vital and dynamic in spirit. A new cause appeared in Brueghel, the cause of simple people in their daily toil, with their joys and sorrows, their hopes and their humor. Brueghel's art championed the life of the individual and contained far reaching moral and social implications.

PLATE XVI

PLATE XVI. GIRL INTERRUPTED AT HER MUSIC. VERMEER

The "Girl Interrupted at Her Music" (Plate XVI) by Vermeer (1632-1675) contains characteristics of light, air and structure defined by the noted English critic, R. W. Wilensky, as architectural painting. While apparently a freely flowing natural presentation, examination reveals that this picture is deliberately planned, all the forms having been arranged in a geometric relationship. It is obvious from the way in which the various objects are foreshortened that perspective had been perfected by this time. Renaissance artists would have been incapable of achieving such effects. Within an *angular perspective* framework, other fundamental procedures, such as the principle of overlapping planes (Fig. 30), are also applied. The placement of the forms is so controlled that all lines move recessively into space, from near to far.

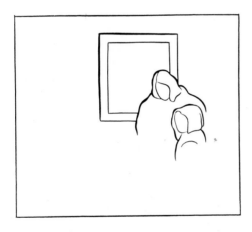

Figure 30. Overlapping Planes

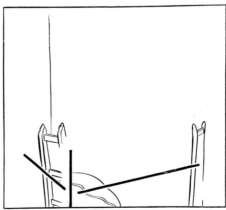

Figure 31. Entrance into Space

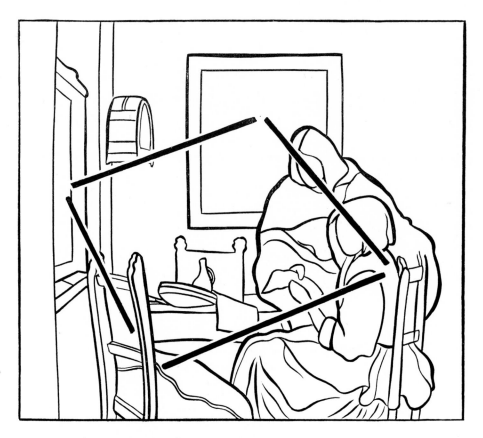

Figure 32. The Completed Enclosure (Vermeer)

Vermeer, like Brueghel, placed the closest form near the bottom of the picture plane, about one-third from its left border (Fig. 31). From here lines diverge *to create expansion with recession*. Within a fragment of the cube (the room) Vermeer placed his forms so as to complete an enclosure of space (a cube within a cube). He obtained this by four sweeping line movements: (1) from the left chair to the girl, (2) to the back wall, (3) to the side window, (4) and back again to the chair (Fig. 32). It is important to note that these lines create an *oblique plane* derived from angular perspective. Many other enclosures may be found in the ingenious interlocking of all the forms within the picture.

Figure 33. Movements in Space (Vermeer)

Figure 33 is a diagram of some of the inner lines of movement and tension in this apparently simple picture. Note the classic whirling spiral. Every form is perfectly placed and directed to obtain a self-contained integrated composition.

Brueghel and Vermeer may be considered the last great representatives of the Flemish school of painting, established by the brothers Van Eyck. Brueghel's painting shows no influence of the chiaroscuro painters of Italy, despite his visit to that country during his youth. At the time of Vermeer's birth, however (1632), the Italian influence had all but obliterated the northern style. Although he never left his home town, Delft, Vermeer still came under the sway of the Italians, whose

93

techniques were carried back to Holland by many Dutch painters who, following the fashion, went to Italy to study. Rembrandt's lineage is directly traceable to Caravaggio, through his Italian trained teachers, although he himself never left his native land.

In contrast to Rembrandt, Vermeer was never completely overwhelmed by the Italian techniques. In spite of his use of chiaroscuro, he may be considered the last great painter in the northern tradition. His work retained its two most dominant characteristics: a love for a luminous, all pervading light, and a mastery of geometric design. His great delicacy in the handling of detail, never vulgarly displayed, conforms to the northern heritage of immaculate craftsmanship. His consciousness of line, while obscured by chiaroscuro, still reflects the tradition of the Van Eycks.

The Flemish painters introduced daylight into painting. Their pictures contained no vacuums of black, so common in the Baroque painting of Italy, where the artist used a beam of light streaming in from an opening in the ceiling to illuminate his subject, which caused the forms to stand out in stark relief against a deeply shadowed background. This is characteristic of Caravaggio or Rembrandt. In contrast to this spot-light illumination, the painters of the north used natural daylight. Vermeer's paintings were enveloped in light which entered through a side window and pervaded the entire room with reflected sunlight. The daylight which the northern painters brought into the picture eventually led to Impressionism.

In this absorption with light and structure Vermeer found a kindred spirit in Cezanne. With both the human interest was subordinate. Vermeer treated his figures impersonally, as a subject upon which lights break and colors play. He was intent on an analysis of pure visual effects. In this sense he was a pure painter whose whole work was devoted to an expression of the wonder of the visual world. His pictures hold no interest for those who look for an illustrated story or human drama.

PLATE XVII

PLATE XVII. VILLAGE AMONG TREES. HOBBEMA

Vermeer remains the pure painter, the painter's painter, concerned solely with the profound drama of light and form in space.

Angular perspective opened the space of the canvas to include the new world which the landscapists of the time were beginning to explore. It furnished the necessary equipment for the interpretation of vast stretches of terrain, the beauty of the countryside, nature in all its moods and glory.

In "Village Among Trees" (Plate XVII) by Hobbema (1638-1709), the 17th century space ideals are clearly visualized. The ground plane has been fitted into the oblique view of angular perspective. The major lines of movement begin with the road at the bottom border, left center, and from there diverge obliquely into space. One line leads to the house at the left, the other follows the road to the right. These divergent lines of movement follow paths comparable in effect to the expanding vision of sight.

But the eye of the observer is not allowed to travel out of the picture, for the road twists inward, its line is picked up by the trees, it circles upward to the tree tops, moves down again, leads back to the house on the left and finally ends at the starting point. This circular movement is the classic whirling spiral which underlines so many of the compositions examined here.

The drawing, "Dutch Landscape With Windmills" (Plate XVIII) by Jan Brueghel (1568-1625), shows how deliberately the artist of the 17th century used the device of expansion. The movement in the picture starts from the near figures on the left, about one-third across the bottom line. From here two basic lines recede into space, one to the left, directed by the horsecart, the other to the right, down the road. This device formed the structural composition of space for many generations to come.

During the 18th and early 19th centuries artists relied for their painting on established techniques, derived from the methods of the old masters. They studied in the museum instead of learning from nature. A great painter like Goya, in this respect, fits into the tradition of chiaroscuro painting. David and Ingres, as leaders of the French academy, attempted to create an art which conformed to the absolute standards of classical form, derived from Raphael and the formalism of the Greeks.

Rebellion against the academy in France found technical equipment and inspiration in Rembrandt and the Dutch. Delacroix, Courbet and Millet may be mentioned as painters who based their art on the chiaroscuro principle of Rembrandt and adapted it for their own expression.

It was during the late 18th and early 19th centuries that landscape painting in a more contemporary form came into being. Constable, in England, went out of doors and examined his immediate environment at first hand. His fresh handling of atmosphere and cool colors startled the art world. At the same time Turner was observing the sunset, the tempest and storm of the sea, examining the possibilities of color as had never been done before. Then there was the Barbizon school, painting the dawn and twilight with poetic mystery. Daubigney and Corot belonged to this school. Finally Daumier, among the first of the expressionists, transformed Rembrandt's technique into paintings which remain unexcelled as human and social commentaries.

All these painters are links in the historical development of painting, leading up to this century. However, they conformed to the spacial conventions of the past. Therefore, after momentary salute to their greatness, we shall return to the main subject under discussion in this work.

PLATE XVIII

Courtesy of The Metropolitan Museum of Art

PLATE XVIII. DUTCH LANDSCAPE WITH WINDMILLS. JAN BRUEGHEL

CHAPTER SEVEN

Aerial Perspective and Impressionism
(19th century)

CHIAROSCURO AND THE LUMINISTIC TRADITION

For over five hundred years (14th to 19th century) perspective was the framework of space in painting. At this point, we shall examine the methods by which artists rendered form within that framework.

In western painting, the first attempts at releasing forms from the flat plane of the picture into the third dimension were made in the 13th and 14th centuries. These efforts culminated in Giotto and the early painters of the Renaissance who modeled from light to dark in emulation of sculpture. Their paintings were solidly established in the third dimension but were hard in outline, the space being devoid of atmosphere.

History accords to Masaccio the honor of being the first painter who softened hard edges and diminished values with distance, to obtain *atmospheric depth*, thereby adding "aerial perspective" to the artist's equipment. Aerial perspective was another step toward the realistic rendering of forms.

The development of aerial perspective from Masaccio to the high Renaissance may be traced in the gradual emergence of modeling by chiaroscuro which replaced sculptured modeling.

Chiaroscuro is the representation of volumes in shapes of light and shadow as they appear when illuminated by a single light source, such as a lamp or a window. This procedure was well established by the time of the Venetian School (17th century), and was crystalized into a formula by Caravaggio and Ribera, the founders of the tradition which reached its heights in the work of Rembrandt.

For purpose of clarification, the term "luminist" defines painters who emphasize light, using a minimum of shadow within the technique of chiaroscuro. One has but to contrast paintings by Titian or Vermeer with Rembrandt to understand what is meant by this term.

The luminists—Titian, Velasquez and Vermeer—established a tradition which led directly to Impressionism. Technically, they are significant because of the masterful way in which they painted forms in *full light*. These painters modeled with glowing colors and diffused edges, which subtly merged into backgrounds in broken tones, giving the effect of forms existing in luminous space.

IMPRESSIONISM

The true fathers of Impressionism were Titian, Velasquez and Vermeer. Culminating peaks, such as Impressionism, which at first glance appear abruptly climactic, have evolved from such seeds sown in the past. Upon close examination the revolutions of Impressionism and modern art are not demonstrations of anarchistic revolt, but rather evolutions of past art forms, modified by advanced knowledge into a contemporary idiom.

Impressionism found the final solution to the problem of aerial perspective posed by luminism. For instance, contrast the earlier masters' knowledge of color and light with the latter. Consider a haystack which Monet painted in his famous "haystack" series (Plate XIX). When asked its color, the earlier painter would have answered "Straw yellow, of course"; and would have painted it that color. But not the impressionist.

Science had now furnished the painter with the theory of the prism, which defines *light and color as synonymous*. It also states that objects are revealed only through the impact of light waves reflecting from them to the observer, and are recognized through color sensation. All colors are composed of variations of the prism.

The impressionist, equipped with this new theory, went out of doors to observe nature at first hand. What he saw was astonishing. He discovered that the sun played magic with the appearance of objects. The haystack, for example, was not necessarily a straw yellow. On the contrary, after Monet studied it, from early dawn to late afternoon, he reported that it was rarely that color. In the early dawn, enveloped in mist, it appeared a low keyed opalescent purple. Where hit by the first beam of sunlight it turned to orange with blue violet shadows. In full light, it was stark yellow; and in the late afternoon it was again orange.

When asked the color of the haystack, the impressionist answered, When? where? under what conditions? He had discovered that *all appearances are conditioned by time and place —by light and atmosphere.*

The impressionist discarded from his palette the old master browns and replaced them with the pure hues of the prism. Instead of mixing colors in solid tones he divided them into component parts and applied them separately on the canvas. In painting trees, for example, he rendered sunlight in patches of blue, green and warm yellow, and shadows in green, blue and violet, with the idea that these colors, when viewed from a distance, would optically merge into an appearance of trees vibrating in light and atmosphere.

The impressionist led the painters out of the museum into the open fields and revealed a world in continuous flux, ever fresh and rejuvenated. An increasing army of disciples, supplied with a palette of the brightest colors, followed him into the countryside. The new movement finally took the world by storm. The "connoisseurs," their noses still glued to museum walls, glancing hostilely at these "upstarts," dubbed them

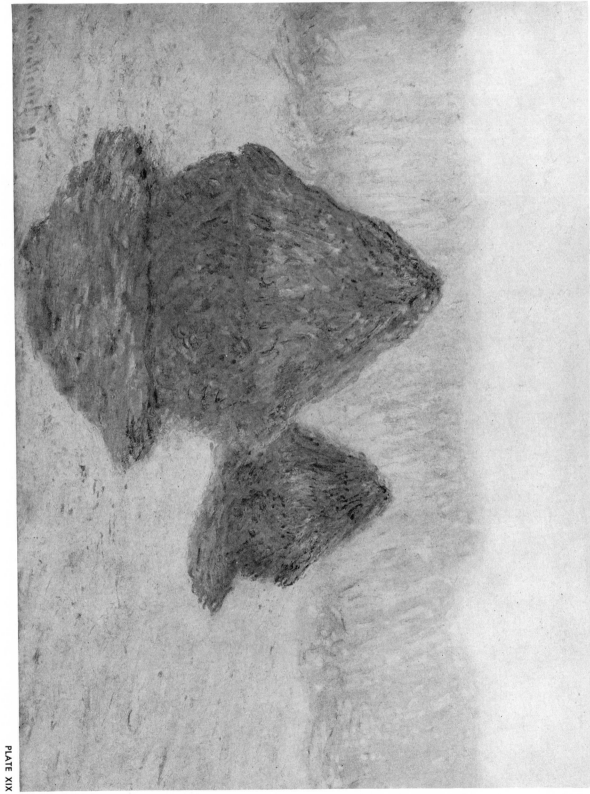

PLATE XIX

PLATE XIX. HAYSTACKS. MONET

"Impressionists" in derision. The name took hold. It is a constant reminder of the struggle that must take place before new ideas can penetrate the inertia of precedent and "irrefutable authority."

But the impressionists had limitations which, from a contemporary viewpoint, loom large. While their use of color was revolutionary, they accepted unquestionably the conventional theories of space. In fact, it may be said that with them perspective reached its ultimate degeneration. To understand this one must contrast their procedure with that of the masters of the Renaissance. The latter constructed space geometrically. Anatomy, drapery, human proportions, the shape of objects were studied directly from nature, but paintings were designed in the studio, the forms being organized in space according to mathematical rule. Theirs was an intellectual process; within perspective space they constructed a formal and integrated art. But not so with the impressionists, who were more intuitive and visual than intellectual. Painting directly from nature, they tried to catch the eternity of a moment. They worked in the heat of enthusiasm to capture and record forever the particular appearance in a moment of time which passes through many changes and is never exactly the same again. Conventional and ordinary compositions were made alive and new only by the excitement of their new vision. Like photographs, their pictures took in only that which their eyes could see from one particular viewpoint. They forgot the function of the picture plane and ignored the concept of forms acting in space, organized within a picture field. The result was a fragment of nature, painted to express the wonder of light and color. It was left for Cezanne to design this awareness into a new spacial order.

Before we continue into the 20th century, we must note the meaning of Impressionism. In contrast to the Medievalists —who conceived of life as the embodiment of an idea—and the Renaissance—which considered life as a concrete, existent fact, established solidly in space—the impressionists believed that the "facts" of life disappeared into a *series of coincidences* relative to time and place. They were the last pictorial link in the evolution of the factual concepts of the Renaissance into the dynamic world of relativity in the 20th century.

CEZANNE AND RENOIR

Technically, Cezanne and Renoir were the artists who summed up the late 19th century. With Renoir, 19th century painting comes to an end; with Cezanne, the 20th century begins.

Renoir's rendering of form is in accord with the theories of the Florentine painter Cennini (1370-?), who wrote in his famous treatise on art that a form in painting can best emulate sculpture when it is high-lighted in the middle and gradually darkened toward the edges. This type of modeling ignores chiaroscuro, which characterizes romantic painting and of which Rembrandt was the greatest exponent.

Renoir was purely classical. His form, based on the Florentine concept and conceived with the sculptured purity of Ingres, was brought up to date by the incorporation of all that was known in his time about color. Surrounding his painting with broken flecks of color, in the manner of the impressionists, he added light, color and air to his classic concept, thereby fulfilling the quest of the luminists. Technically speaking, Renoir concludes a whole cycle in art from the Renaissance through the 19th century.

Cezanne, on the other hand, made a definite break with the past. He was concerned with visual space. He drew from Impressionism a new concept of form and space, interpreted through color plane relationships. Cezanne inaugurated the classicism of the 20th century.

CHAPTER EIGHT

New Vision of Space

PAUL CEZANNE (1839-1906)

Paul Cezanne was a painter's painter, a pure painter who devoted his life to the discovery of a *pictorial equivalent* to the world as he saw it and intuitively knew it to be. His spirit was that of the analyst, his search that of the scientist. His work is a synthesis of vision, intellect and emotion, resulting in an order where every part is related to the whole, every emotional reaction deliberately controlled for the overall effect.

Cezanne's paintings are unpicturesque, his subjects commonplace. Any motif was suitable for his quest. His backyard, his studio, the countryside, a plate of fruit on the table—everything he saw excited his enthusiasm, inspired his creative urge, assumed prime importance as a display of the magical world of color and space to which he was as sensitively attuned as the musician is to sound. His unique genius lay in the fact that what he saw contributed to the new understanding of space as developed in our century.

Cezanne's art, devoid of literary content, may disconcert the observer who can enjoy a picture only when it tells a story. This type of "connoisseur," who enthusiastically "follows the exhibits," may be taken aback, look blankly at the homely work and secretly wonder where its value lies. He may be further perplexed by finding so many of the pictures unfinished, mere fragments. Cezanne was an uneven painter who sought desperately, and often unsuccessfully, to "realize his sensations."

He threw many of his canvases away in complete despair over his inability "to realize." Yet all the pictures which survived have long since been gobbled up by the dealers, and can now be found in great collections and museums.

This mild-mannered recluse, conservative and catholic in faith, painted pictures which shook the foundations of the academic fortress and touched off the epic struggle of modern art. The core of this revolution may be found, of all places, in Cezanne's apparently innocent looking still-lifes, which seem to be arranged geometrically but appear completely disjointed when contrasted with paintings of the past. Their forms are off kilter. Lines of tables, for instance, do not connect; and planes diverge instead of converging. They appear as a series of individual facets, like the parts of a jigsaw puzzle which somehow are not assembled into any previously known order.

We could assume, of course, that Cezanne did not know how to apply even the most elementary laws of perspective (which any youngster learns in the early grades and soon uses satisfactorily). In reality he was pioneering in a new direction, searching for the pictorial equivalent of a new principle of optics. His famous still-lifes are the articulation of a new perceptual awareness, as important to the contemporary painter as the optics of perspective were to the Renaissance. It is with this in mind that his still-lifes have been selected for analysis.

CEZANNE AND THE IMPRESSIONISTS

Before venturing into a study of Cezanne's paintings, let us enter with him into the early 20th century, when he first became known. By 1900, the impressionists were reaping the full harvest of popularity. Cezanne never shared in their success. He took from them his basic color equipment and theory—but, conscious of their shortcomings, he accepted none of their conclusions as final. He went to nature to explore on his own, with occasional visits to the museums for inspirational guidance. Contrary to the impressionists, he learned from the masters about the necessity for structure and organization. But he discovered from nature that their concepts could not fit into his modern world.

By this time Impressionism came dangerously close to establishing a standardized creed of painting and becoming academic. Gauguin, Van Gogh, Seurat also learned all that could be gotten from the impressionists and immediately adopted the new theory to their own ends (Plate XX). But of all these 19th century painters, Cezanne was the only one who dared to investigate the validity of perspective. Taking no precedent for granted, he ventured into hitherto unexplored realms of optics and came back with the startling discovery that the way we see does not necessarily coincide with perspective law!

For his experiments, Cezanne set up a bowl of fruit and folded a napkin or tablecloth on a table. These he examined with a clear eye and mind, completely ignoring preconceived ideas as to how the things should look. He studied the relationship of objects as perceived through color planes and movements. He became conscious of their monumentality as they ranged themselves in space, held in place by the tensions of gravity, and expressed through symbols of light and color. Through his telescopic eye the forms assumed gigantic proportions; the napkin and table cloth appeared like mountain ranges on the table top, which held them solidly in space. He strove to express the vitality inherent in all of nature's manifestations. In his study he found the harmony of the universe, and pioneered toward the new space awareness as we understand it today. In this sense his paintings contain the thought content, the metaphysics of our age.

CEZANNE AND PERSPECTIVE

In pre-Renaissance art the picture plane served as a *mirror* which reflected man's ideals. From the Renaissance to this cen-

PLATE XX

Courtesy of The Art Institute of Chicago

PLATE XX. THE BEDROOM AT ARLES. VAN GOGH

tury, it functioned as a *window* unfolding an event or a scene. The latter day "realists," like the camera, recorded art in true perspective which, they thought, had solved for all time the riddle of portraying upon a flat surface the appearance of objects as they existed in space.

Cezanne was the first painter to look into hitherto unexplored realms of optics and discover areas of perception beyond the boundaries of the perspective theory. He expounded a new form concept which anticipated contemporary science and recent psychological findings pertaining to vision. For clarification of this a discussion of the camera will be found pertinent.

HUMAN VISION AND PERSPECTIVE

The camera is scientifically constructed after the mechanism of the human eye. It is supposed to record objects truly and really as seen. It will therefore be used to demonstrate how untrue this may be when related to sight.

One of the obvious discrepancies between the vision of the eyes and that of the camera is that the eyes see stereoscopically, which enables them to perceive roundness more correctly, while the photo records in flat silhouetted images. Yet, the differences between three dimensional space vision and the flat silhouette of the photograph does not seem to have aroused, in the minds of contemporary realists, the suspicion that human vision and the camera do not coincide.

Further, the camera instantaneously includes all things within one field of vision, with a preconditioned, fixed and concentrated focus. The eyes, on the other hand, have a much more limited and, at the same time, complex view of things. The eyes see *not more than one object at one time,* and can only focus upon *particular points of that object.* They take in the whole object in a roving look, in a series of *individual views.* They see more like a movie camera, recording objects in space in an infinite number of images which the mind pieces together to complete an idea of the whole. In this process memory plays an important part.

A movie camera which could take pictures stereoscopically, and in full color, would approach human vision more closely than any mechanical instrument invented to date. The differences between the still photo and the motion picture are vast. Yet, contemporary painting based on camera perspective portrays much the same experience as that derived from a still photo.

To demonstrate further that camera perspective is a theoretical device for picture making, not necessarily true to vision, we must consider the differences between a photo recording of certain events and the way they are actually seen. Suppose a vase is set close to a window, through which can be seen the houses across the street and the activities on the sidewalk below. In photographing this subject the camera would have the following alternatives: (a) with a general focus, it could record the whole view with everything equally defined by chiaroscuro; (b) the focus could be centered on the vase, which then would be recorded sharply, and the rest of the subject, *out of focus,* would come out blurred; or, (c) by focusing upon the background, it would become sharply defined and the vase would appear blurred.

Now let us study the same subject and *consciously recognize* how we see. By coming close to the vase and concentrating the eyes upon it we see it standing large and round in space relief, but the view through the window goes through a visual shrinking process, due to the fact that it is *out of focus* and the separate images are not properly synchronized in the cerebellum. Next we focus on the houses and the street. By shifting vision in this manner a strange thing happens: the view expands to its true size, but the vase appears as a *double image.* This is due to the fact that we see with two eyes, which results in two pictures (one for each eye). The two views become unified into one image in the brain only through mutual focus on an object. When out of focus the two images do not synchronize but overlap and are seen as split, or, double images.

Another way of verifying this experiment is to place a finger close between the eyes. First focus both eyes on the finger, then focus on the background, then close each eye alternately and look at the finger with the other eye. Note the shifting images as the eyes move from the finger to the background and back again. Observe that when looking at the background the finger appears double. When you look at the finger with each eye alternately, it appears to jump from side to side. *Each change of focus results in a new view very different from the others.*

The implications are far reaching. They show that in the field of binocular vision there is much that is beyond the boundaries of any previously known visual practice in art. They indicate that seeing may become a marvelous adventure in awareness, and that, if one but learns to really see with the eyes, new areas of visual perception may become sources of inspiration.

THE MIND'S EYE

Vision is defined as the recognition of objective phenomena by means of color-light sensation. The eyes are the organs through which this transpires, reality being recognized only by the mind. In the final analysis, recognition of objects (seeing) is a physical—plus mental—process, with emotional overtones. Psychological reactions to the familiar or to the unknown, plus selection based on emotional response to the beauty of one form for its quality of suggested line, color or texture, and the total disregard of another for the same reasons, is bound to lead to what may appear a distortion of the factual. This awareness of the distortion of objects as they are perceived by the senses, is of vital concern to the artist, if he is to interpret life as a living experience and not as a phenomenon of mechanistic principles.

The pictorial possibilities of expressing the visions of the "mind's eye" are boundless. However, the physical limitations of the picture must be considered. This compares with the musical score which although circumscribed yet offers infinite opportunity, limited only by the creative range of the artist. It has been observed how the artists of the past created great art within their limitations. Visual perception, as defined by the new awareness of space, has resulted in an art as different from previous art forms as our century differs from the past.

THE PSYCHOLOGICAL FACTOR OF RECOGNITION

There is a definite distinction between *how* we see and *what* we see. *How* we see is mechanical law (perspective). *What* we see depends on psychological conditioning. It is a learned process. We *learn* to recognize through definition, training and predilection. The process of recognition is *psychological*. In our capacity to recognize we sum up all our knowledge, including that which lies deeply hidden in the unknown realms of our consciousness.

The eyes are mechanical instruments. They project an infinite number of individual images upon the retina which the mind *pieces together* in order to perceive the picture as a whole. In this process two instruments are functioning, the eyes and the mind. The eyes *see* and the mind *recognizes*, memory playing its functional part. This factor of recognition (interpretation by the mind) is involved in the principle of the *focal horizontal*, now to be examined in Cezanne's "Basket of Apples."

THE FOCAL HORIZONTAL

The painting "Basket of Apples" by Cezanne (Plate XXI) incorporates the new fields of visual perception. To emphasize

PLATE XXI

PLATE XXI.   THE BASKET OF APPLES.   CEZANNE

what has happened, contrast the table in this painting with that of Vermeer's (Plate XVI). Like Vermeer, Cezanne set his table a short distance back from the picture plane; it is upon, and around it, that the action takes place.

Cezanne's table has been broken into planes whose shape and placement in space are determined by (1) facet vision, (2) psychological recognition and the resultant focal horizontal, and (3) the recessive diagonal.

Vermeer's table is an optical distortion of fact. Whatever its perspective, the mind *knows* that it is rectangular and hori-

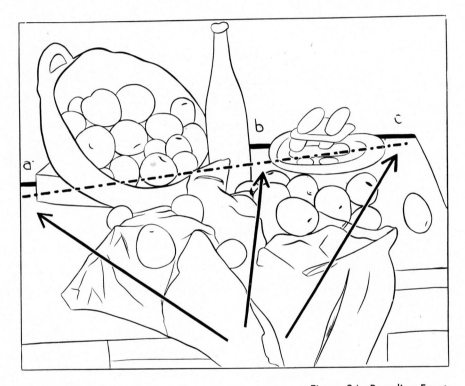

Figure 34. Receding Facets

zontal with the floor and earth. If *recognized* as otherwise, one's gravitational sense would be thrown off balance. In viewing objects, the mind must instantly *recognize* true geometric shape and relationship in space. This must ensue—despite optical distortion caused by the mechanics of vision—otherwise the world would result in chaos. This discrepancy, between optical distortion and known truth, Cezanne resolved in his painting as follows:

It has been observed that the eyes can concentrate on only *one area* at a time. They see in facets. Obviously, Cezanne in observing the back lines of the table top (Fig. 34), first looked at "a," then moved to "b" and finally to "c." When his eyes focused on "a" his mind instantly recognized that line as horizontal. The same with "b" and "c." However, "b" and "c" were progressively farther back in space from "a." Their placement in the space of the picture was conditioned by the length of the line of distance between them and the nearest projection (the napkin). Therefore, the composite of "a," "b" and "c" was visualized pictorially like this _ — ‾ . Note that while each facet retains its recognized horizontalness, in relation to each other they are all placed in space along the line of a *recessive diagonal.*

This interpretation of vision as the multiple faceted appearance of objects existing in space introduces a new theory in painting. Cezanne's breakdown of form is not arbitrary, but rooted in the facts of sight.

From it is derived the principle of the focal horizontal. This means that whatever part of a horizontal line the eyes rest upon it is instantly recognized as horizontal, in total disregard of perspective. Cezanne obtains the recession of the table into space by an *implied diagonal* which moves from facet to facet, as the eyes move along in a series of steps, one above the other, into space. But each facet retains its focal, recognized horizontalness.

From this is derived the pictorial principle that there are three basic line movements: the vertical, which runs parallel with the vertical plane of the canvas and is *inactive;* the horizontal, which runs parallel with the bottom border of the picture and retains the character of *rest,* or *focus;* and the diagonal, which is the action line, the line that the eye follows as it moves from the horizontal and the vertical picture plane into the depth of the canvas.

These visual truths are related to the principle of the cube. In modern art, psychological awareness merges with the cube into the new theory of pictorial space first introduced by Cezanne.

RHYTHMS IN SPACE

"Les Grosses Pommes" by Cezanne (Plate XXII) contains more of his revolutionary doctrine of space. A cursory view of this painting leaves no disturbing effect of dislocated objects. Only on close examination does it become apparent that the lines of the table do not join into a continuous curve but are, instead, broken (Fig. 35). Furthermore, the large plate

Figure 35. Rhythms in Space

on which the fruits are placed is not completed, but left a half circle.

Cezanne chose, from his view, only those *facets* which fitted into a rhythmic scheme. His subject is a design composed of three half circles. He abstracted lines and planes from natural form and released them to function independently for purposes of rhythmic design, thereby making another break with the past.

The saucer is divided into two sections by the cup and apple (see page 116 for theory of split image), each part visualized as a circular plane moving back into space individually. Again, the flat cardboard on the table, behind the cup (Fig. 36), is split into distinct facets, the movements working contrapuntally. Picasso and Braque found this a source for departures into abstract facet painting.

The circular movement of the composition is completed in the lower right hand corner, where Cezanne separated the reflection of the plate from its natural place and twisted it to force the eye back into the picture space. The back wall is divided into a severe rectangle and square, which contrast with the sweeping curves of the table. He deliberately separated planes from their places in nature and utilized them abstractly for pictorial structure. He selected lines and planes for rhythm and movement, assembled into a dynamic pictorial order.

This picture avows the modern doctrine of liberation from the conventions of natural appearances. By releasing planes and lines from nature and letting them function as symbols of dynamic movement in space, it charted the course of modern art. However, this particular still life may be considered as not too well integrated. The picture contains the core, not the fulfilment of his objectives. Cezanne had made a great discovery.

To recapitulate: In this painting all the forms are derived from nature, which supplied the motif and inspiration. But Cezanne utilized nature not as a subject to copy, but as a point of departure. He attempted to interpret sensory reaction to color vibrations, which in themselves contain dynamic-spacial equivalents to natural forces.

Here, for the first time since the Renaissance, an artist deliberately freed the elements (lines, planes and colors) from their traditional appearance and utilized them abstractly as

PLATE XXII

Collection of Jakob Goldschmidt

PLATE XXII. LES GROSSES POMMES. CEZANNE

forces which in themselves contain rhythm and harmony, the language of the universe.

As a choreographer Cezanne was possibly equal to Giotto. Where the latter concentrated on man, the former was concerned mainly with the drama of form in space. He arranged his apples as carefully as Giotto did his human figures. Both painters belonged to the same religion; both were devout Catholics. The wide range between their subject matter demonstrates the different ways of interpreting life by men of art.

Figure 36. Contrapuntal Movement

Cezanne, like Giotto and Brueghel, viewed life as a dramatic spectacle. With the latter humanity was the actor, with Cezanne it was the forces of nature. Cezanne was inspired not by religion, or human tragedy, but by the wonders of the visual world. In this sense his paintings are profoundly emotional. They contain love and reverence. The tenderness inspired by an apple, as revealed in space and glorified by light and color, led one writer to state that there is as much spirituality in an apple by Cezanne as in a Raphael madonna. With Cezanne inanimate nature took on spiritual significance. To him, as to Van Gogh, all nature was sanctified by the "light of the Lord." In this sense his paintings present a drama as profoundly moving as any that may be found in art.

It is suggested that the reader study the "Pot of Geraniums and Fruit" (Plate XXIII) for the arrangement of planes on the table top, the movement of folds in the table cloth and the organization of the apples distributed within the different areas. Note how Cezanne divided the background with contrasted dark leaves against the light wall and light leaves against the dark wall. Follow the movement of planes, where every area is carefully defined by color strokes, reflecting his sensitive response to light and color as symbols of space.

THE SPACE LINE

Cezanne's use of line and color to model form was revolutionary. His color has led many writers to ignore his functional line, which was the starting point for excursions into abstraction in art.

We noted before how Cezanne freed lines from objects and allowed them to function as rhythmic forces. We now direct our attention to his use of lines to emphasize the voluminous existence of forms in space.

Many of the forms in Cezanne's paintings are shaped by lines which function, not to define contour (shapes of objects), but rather as vacuums, voids of space out of which objects build up into full roundness. They are the negative factors against which forms assert themselves as positive forces. Cezanne employed the principle that when the eyes focus on a form, it completely absorbs their capacity for color recognition; and therefore the space around it appears negative, devoid of color. Rouault's line functions much in the same way; like a leading in stained glass, it shapes forms. He learned from Cezanne (and

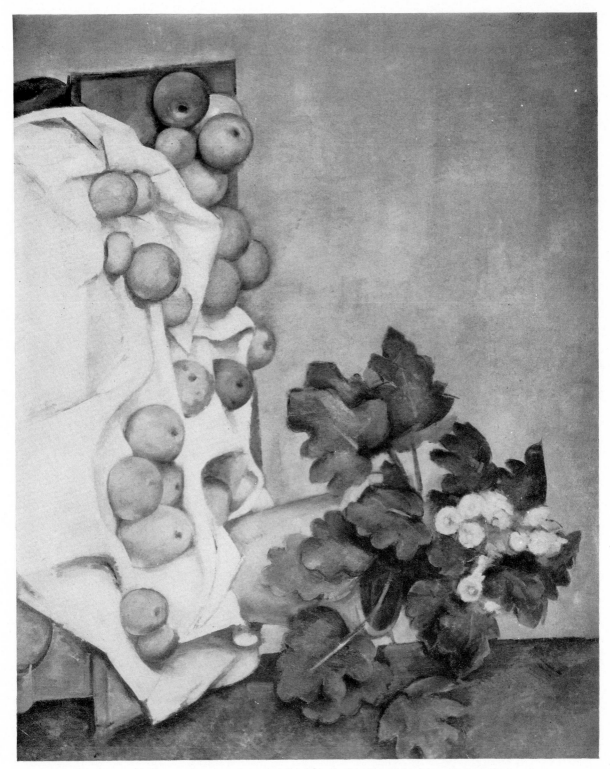

PLATE XXIII

Collection of Mr. and Mrs. Sam A. Lewisohn

PLATE XXIII. POT OF GERANIUMS AND FRUIT. CEZANNE

by his work with stained glass) that pigments, no matter how intense, are infinitely weak when compared with nature. Therefore, to approximate nature's intensity the artist must resort to liberties (distortion). These painters, acutely sensitive to the intensities of color, enhanced their brilliance by a black space behind the object in order to obtain the greatest contrast possible with paint. This procedure has been verified by contemporary psychological research into laws of visual perception.

FUNCTIONAL COLOR

Cezanne grew out of Impressionism, which opened the paths he was to follow alone. He was as sensitive to color nuance as the musician is to sound. He responded intensely to all vibrations of color and light. In this respect he resembled a wireless photo, where impulses are sent through the air to be collected on a flat surface as dots, which, through correct size and distribution, take on the shape and semblance of the recorded object. Cezanne's little mosaics of color were not intellectually formulated, like Seurat's. They derived from minute study and direction observation. Nothing in nature was taken for granted. It has to be approached with humility and reverence. Its beauties had to be sought out and expressed. Formulas are the equipment of the creatively sterile. For the creative mind they are the instruments with which he explores the unknown, to bring back knowledge which destroys formulas. Cezanne's knowledge never blocked his inspiration and theory always gave way to direct observation.

The formula available to Cezanne was the prism. He searched nature for its verification. He saw the world as revealed through light. In his painting, every stroke was a separate color, every color a plane, and planes shaped into volumes which, through correct delineation, took on a resemblance to objects existing in nature. In this respect it must be emphasized that Cezanne, in painting his apple, never considered it as such, but rather as a form revealed to him through light and color vibrations. It was the color of form in space that excited his creativity. He never tried to describe objects in their ordinary appearance.

The impressionists employed the principle of the prism to portray light and atmosphere. Cezanne used it to express volume. The colors of the prism are arranged in order from yellow as the lightest to blue and violet as the darkest. Cezanne incorporated this arrangement into his modeling of form. He superimposed the prismatic order on the red of the apple, or the white of the tablecloth or the face. In a portrait, for example, the light side was rendered in yellow, orange and red, and the shaded side in green, blue and violet, the local color being sacrificed to the creation of volume with the colors of the prism.

By modeling form with pure color symbols derived from the prism, Cezanne supplied a new concept to replace the outmoded chiaroscuro. As he released the line from the object and abstracted it for rhythmic movement, so also he released color and made it function abstractly, to express volume and space.

The use of pure prismatic colors for the modeling of form naturally created a cleavage with the past. It dated the old masters, whose works are milestones on the road of progress, whose spirit of creativity is timeless, but whose idea of form is relegated to history. The young painter today must learn from Cezanne if he wants to create in the idiom of his century.

CHAPTER NINE

Abstract Art

NEW FORM CONCEPTS

Cezanne's visualization of form as a series of planes, each a unit of vision expressed through color vibration and moving in an individual orbit within a field of space, creating the whole by an integration of related parts, was the basis for a new philosophy concerning the construction of a picture.

The cubists, direct heirs of Cezanne, explored the ramifications of the object in its multiple aspects, combining several viewpoints simultaneously into a single structure. Like chemists, they broke down form, dissolved it into planes, released its energy. In this process the external aspect of the object disappeared and became just barely recognizable by tactile surface characteristics which were sometimes retained for descriptive and aesthetic effects.

The modern world is no longer factual in its interpretation of the object. In contrast to the Renaissance, where the object was considered a solid fact, it has today dissolved into a force, a space enclosing a quantity of energy. Ours is an era whose dimension has extended to include the invisible world of dynamics. It is in this area that the realities of life are now determined. This has changed the whole concept of existence. The meaning of life has been transformed by the microscope, the spectrum and the engineer's graph. Parallel with this extension of the realities of existence, the modern artist has penetrated beyond the surfaces of objects to analyze their inner

PLATE XXIV

Collection, The Museum of Modern Art, New York

PLATE XXIV. ROAD NEAR ESTAQUE. BRAQUE

structural dynamics. From here he went on to the picture problem, explored *pictorial dynamics,* and revolutionized painting.

In this quest Picasso, Braque, Kandinsky and finally Mondrian reached out beyond Cezanne to express the contemporary world through art. They endeavored to merge the new philosophy with principles basic to the picture. As the anthropologists went to the primitives to find fundamental facts pertaining to the character of man, these modern painters explored the art of the African, the Indian and prehistoric man in an effort to reestablish a fundamental language of painting, in a form characteristic of this century.

These original thinkers have been absorbed with the problem of space — not as defined by the camera, but rather space that the picture encloses and that the mind speculates upon and feels free to roam as it seeks to express life. They reestablished basic laws of painting. Cezanne released art from the imitation of sculptured form and the perspective of the Renaissance. They were free to create a new symbolic language. In their quest for purification of the picture they stripped art of extraneous subject matter (literary content). From simple objects such as a table, a banjo, a newspaper, a vase, or with abstract lines, planes and colors, they constructed forms on their canvas. They took from the visual world only those elements which fit into their picture, by which process objects became transformed, reappearing as a series of related dynamic lines, color planes and textures, constructed into a design.

Organization, construction, design — this is what these artists were seeking. As a result of their efforts the modern artist now possesses the elements of a new plastic language. Lines, color planes, textures, organization, design, structure — the basis for a new order. Art streamlined, stripped bare of all unessentials, cleared of all extraneous matter; that is what they were after, and that is what they obtained.

Braque (1881-   ) painted the "Road Near Estaque" (Plate XXIV) at the age of twenty-seven, in 1908, two years after Cezanne's death. It shows how thoroughly he had learned his lesson from Cezanne. Braque conceived his picture as a volume of space occupied by solid forms, held together by tensions and built up by strokes of color planes. Observe the recession of the wall and the series of flat planes moving back into distance together. Braque attempted to construct space as a solid unit of functional blocks where, as in a building the removal of one block would collapse the whole structure. Observe also his use of the functional line to strengthen the existence of the forms. The picture demonstrates how Cezanne's disciples intellectually synthesized and formulated into a system the concepts of line, color and space which the master had discovered in his pioneering search to "realize his sensations." This picture is of historical interest as a step in the building of modern art.

ANALYTICAL CUBISM: THE ANATOMY OF SPACE

Cubism is generally considered dated, having occupied the minds of its progenitors, Picasso and Braque, for only a few years. The two painters retired to their studios between 1909 and 1912 to break down form and study its mechanism. In this process objects were completely dismembered and the line, the dynamic symbol of movement, was used as the instrument for dissection. Like a surgeon's knife, it cut through the surface of the object to get at its underlying structure, its basic import, the energy of its existence.

The cubists' spirit is comparable to that of the anatomist of the Renaissance, who sought knowledge of the human figure by penetrating beyond its surface for a study of its structure.

PLATE XXV

PLATE XXV. DRAWING. PICASSO

The cubists were also anatomists, not of muscles, but of the dynamics of space. They smashed form to release its energies.

The cubists were confronted with the problem of portraying their new idea on the flat surface of the canvas. They had no precedent for their new theory of representing multiple space. It demanded much experimentation and laboratory research.

The drawing by Picasso (Plate XXV) offers a key to cubism. This study consists only of lines and textures. All external resemblance to the object drawn has been eliminated to the extent that it is not recognizable. He *selected* only those of its lines which express dimension, gravitational stress, tensions, axes of movement, so related as to compose a structure of *energies in space*. They are the aesthetic counterpart to the engineer's graph, an analysis of weight tensions and dynamics. Can it be said that this drawing of the forces which underly a structure is less "realistic" than one which offers merely surface description? The cubists were trying to render visually the inner realities revealed by science.

In the drawing (Plate XXVI), Picasso has again attempted the dynamic analysis of a form, apparently a human figure. In this case the weights and space structure are symbolized mostly by flat planes. The head is abstracted into a sphere, loosely supported by a tipped horizontal plane (the shoulders). Two vertical planes describe the dimension and space of the torso and are supported by two other vertical planes with an implication of volume (the legs), and a third plane in the rear which represents a further gravitational pull of the weight of the body into the earth. This drawing is a speculative analysis of the *space displacement* of the different forms which compose the human body.

The fulfillment of the cubist idea is found in "The Poet" (Plate XXVII). In this painting *space forms* are expressed in their entirety, evolving into a structure extremely complex, entirely dynamic — and to a degree confusing. The picture is electrified with lines and planes moving through space. Within this maze of active forces the "poet" gradually emerges. From many views of his body one form appears, with arms, torso, neck and a multiple faceted head.

The confusion in this picture results from the attempt to portray many aspects of a form (front, back and side) on the flat surface of the canvas. To obtain this, the object first had to be divided into facets. These were flattened out as planes and then reassembled into a volume of picture space where they were presented frontally, that is, parallel with the picture plane. Their construction in space *derives from the cube principle.* They overlap for recession and move horizontally, vertically and diagonally within the enclosure.

Why is this picture entitled "The Poet"? Is Picasso trying to be sardonic? Presumably, the person who sat "to be dismembered" was a poet. Suggestions of his face, nose, mouth and moustache are incorporated into the upper facets, where a tilted pipe also emerges with a degree of humor. The title has many implications. Is not a poet also a "construction in space," composed of dynamic physical forces?

Besides, Picasso may be stating ambiguously and with some amusement that if one needs a title to a picture, why, here it is. It could as well have been called "A Study in Dynamic Space Form."

Through cubism Picasso and Braque established a system to interpret the anatomy of space. Their paintings, now fully accepted by the museums, are not only works of art in their own rights, but also historic landmarks in the evolution of space form in the art of this century.

SYNTHETIC CUBISM: THE ANATOMY OF THE PICTURE

After their analysis of space-form, Picasso and Braque next directed their attention to an analysis of the picture. They

PLATE XXVI

PLATE XXVI. DRAWING. PICASSO

PLATE XXVII

PLATE XXVII.   THE POET.   PICASSO

felt that analytical cubism emulated sculpture (volume) at the expense of decoration, and therefore decided that the picture plane should serve not only as a point of departure into depth, but also as a surface to be ornamented.

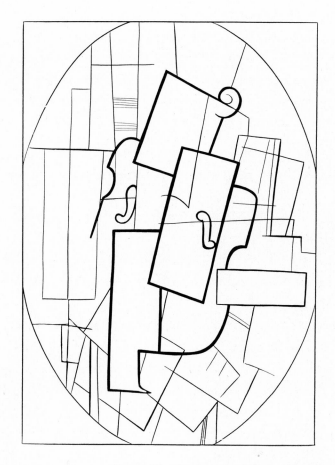

Figure 37. The Animated Picture Plane

With this in mind these painters evolved the idea of reassembling facets into flat patterned design. In this process they again utilized the principle of recession derived from the cube. The planes were arranged vertically (parallel with the picture plane) and overlapped for recession into space. They were conceived as cutouts constructed into an order.

In his "Oval Still Life" (Plate XXVIII), Braque arranged the composition within a shallow depth, the planes being closer than ever to the picture surface (Fig. 37). He lifted facets of violin, newspaper, cloth and table from the horizontal plane (as they existed in nature) to a vertical position to achieve a harmonious design on the picture plane. In this phase the artist also became aware of ornamentation as an essential part of decoration. He abstracted quality and texture from objects and arranged them contrapuntally for maximum aesthetic effect.

THE FUNCTIONAL PICTURE PLANE

Picasso emerged from his laboratory with a complete mastery of his medium and a new concept of art. Restated principles of aesthetics, formal order, pictorial space, pattern design and color harmony resulted in a series of paintings, of which Plate XXIX is an example.

Picasso's space is not derived from mathematics (as with the masters of the past), but from a realization that the world is a visual field, revealed through the mind (consciousness), where all existence is translated into images which reflect one's awareness of life and the universe in which it transpires. Perspective plays no part in this connection.

In "The Red Table Cloth" (Plate XXIX) the picture plane functions, not as a window looking out on nature, but as a surface on which ideas are expressed through the medium of paint. Cezanne's paintings contain little mosaics of color, the results of which are comparable to the excitement caused on the retina by the infinite impulses of energy emanating from objects in nature. Through this maze he searched for rule and order. Picasso completed Cezanne's intuitive search. This may be summarized as follows:

PLATE XXVIII

Collection, The Museum of Modern Art, New York

PLATE XXVIII. OVAL STILL LIFE. BRAQUE

Man functions creatively to the extent that he interprets sensory reactions in intelligible terms.

Contemporary man views experience as a series of dynamic relationships, any situation serving as focus in a long sequence of events between cause and effect.

To express life in contemporary terms a painting must incorporate movement (action), time (duration of action), and space (place of action), without which experience in life — or art — is inconceivable.

This space-time connotation is expressed in art by line, plane and color symbols which, through correct juxtaposition, interpret the multiple-faceted experience of contemporary living. As life is never static, but moves in a continual reshuffling of patterns creating an ever changing order of relationships, so a painting must also incorporate, within its focus, a sense of dynamic order in a pattern of rhythmic and harmonious form movement in space.

To understand the techniques devised to express this hypothesis, view the subject of this still life (Plate XXIX) as through a window. The traditional artist would *penetrate* the window and would paint the objects he sees, as they are related to each other in perspective. However, if a painter defined the outline of the objects *on the window pane* with a black line, the window pane would then function as the picture plane. The shapes would form a pattern resulting in a decorative picture. In this procedure the painter would have to remain in a stationary position relative to the view. If he moved from one place to another, the view on the window pane would change with his movement. If he outlined the areas created by the objects on the window pane as they "followed his movement," he would be tracing their movement relative to him. Tracing moving objects such as an automobile, train, or a running person would have the same result.

The possibility of portraying objects "moving in space" is a result of *facet vision* and is the complete opposite of the photographic image (which is a remembered assemblage of the whole). Innumerable views (facets) are offered for selection, from which Picasso, in his painting, chose only those which marked upon the picture plane areas enclosing *orbits of movement in space*. These facets furnished the space motif for his picture, functioning as (1) symbols of negative space (space enclosing objects); and (2) positive space, where the facts of the object are shown through characteristic shapes, gestures, color and texture. Harmonized as lines and planes, colors and patterns, they were finally integrated into a design.

The abstract artist feels privileged to dislocate planes from their place in nature and shape them on the picture plane for movement and design. He can lay them flat, for a hori-

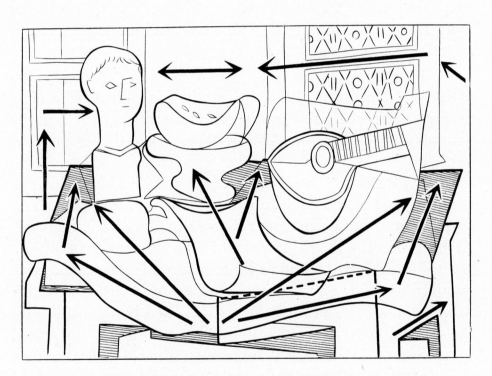

Figure 38. Movements in Space (Abstraction)

PLATE XXIX

PLATE XXIX.   THE RED TABLE CLOTH.   PICASSO

zontal movement into depth, or lift them vertically, for a vertical design relationship. The lifting of the horizontal plane, as it exists in nature, to a vertical position, and superimposing it upon the picture plane for decoration, marks the evolution from naturalism to abstraction.

This brings us again to the table top (Fig. 38), which in "The Red Table Cloth" is definitely related to Cezanne. The planes in Picasso's painting serve a multiple function: (1) they portray placement in space from several views, (2) they are keyed in color to relate harmoniously and (3) they design shapes on the picture plane, in this way combining plastic elements and decoration into a dynamic structure. This ingenious weaving of plastic space and decoration into a unified design assumes the stature of classical order, revealing the mastery of Picasso at his best.

Throughout the picture Picasso played positive and negative space against each other. Each plane in itself was ornamented for variation and texture. Note the contrapuntal play of the facets of the table cloth, the realistic rendering of the pearl ornamentation on the mandolin, and the lines on the page of music, all abstracted for excitement and variation. All the lines, planes, colors and space forms are designed in this way for aesthetic purposes. Distinctly linked to nature, they result from a careful analysis of the objective world.

After years of devious excursions through cubism, the painter of the 20th century has emerged with a new symbolic language to interpret the spectacle of life as an array of dynamically related forces, whose impact produces a series of indelible imprints on the senses. His interpretation depends on his own creative knowledge and capacity to respond. In Picasso, this flows into an art form where the canvas contains the illusion of a field of space occupied by images which interpret an emotional awareness of the vitality, rhythm and harmony inherent in all life's manifestations.

MOVEMENT IN TIME AND SPACE

The portrayal of the multiple aspect of the object in space is not new in art. To emphasize its positive merits, camera vision will again be used for comparison. The photograph is the instantaneous recording of an image; a flash recording of an event, catching the fragment of a second out of eternity. Its limitations are demonstrated by the fact that, to take a photo, action must usually be suspended and time held up for the duration of the exposure. The still photo, therefore, must necessarily be static. Even if the object is taken in action, the element of movement in time is destroyed through the instantaneous nature of its recording. This is most evident in photos taken of violent action, such as football games or races. The figures, caught in transit, seem frozen. The same quality characterizes impressionistic painting where, parallel with the development of the camera, the artist sought instantaneity — catching the fleeting moment of nature, the momentary effect of light on the object. Time became an important consideration in painting.

This analysis of the moment, the study of appearances as a series of instantaneous occurences, each an individual recording, a unique effect, a different picture, opened a new field for the artist to explore. It expressed a further break with the fixed and static concepts of the Renaissance. By examining nature in all its manifold appearances, it made possible the multiple vision in modern art.

The analogy between the photo and the painting holds in the further development, where the photographer, by learning to multiply his recording in a series of pictures of an event which, pieced together and flashed in sequence, gave the illusion of time and movement, resulting in the motion picture, also applies to painting, where the artist, out of the instantaneous and momentary recording of the impressionist, developed a concept which included, in one picture, a composite of nature in its multiple appearances.

PLATE XXX

PLATE XXX. LE VELODROME. METZINGER

The consideration of movement, or duration in time and space, to express animation is not new in art, as can readily be seen in the art of ancient Greece, where the artist most subtly evaded the static by expressing, in his statuary, the continuity of a movement from its start to its finish. The pose is not static, photographic, but rather the embodiment of the many ramifications of a movement, so subtly combined as to contain within the frozen pose of the statue an implication of continuous flux, of rhythmically undulating movement, animating the cold stone and imparting to it life, a sense of self contained existence. The imitators of the Greeks, the Romans, and later, the neo-classicists of the 19th century, being realistic in concept and ignorant of the subtle distortion of the Greeks — wherein the secret to their rhythm lay — endeavored to obtain movement through violent gesture, but obtained only petrified poses, demonstrating thereby that movement in art can only be expressed through the duration of motion within time and not by catching the movement of a single gesture, no matter how violent the pose.

DERIVATIVE PAINTING

The picture "Le Velodrome" (Plate XXX), by Metzinger (1883-   ) utilizes cubist techniques for literary content. In contrast to Picasso and Braque, whose main search was for formality and structure, Metzinger obviously devoted his techniques to subject matter, in this case, a bicycle race. These different approaches to, and utilization of art, divide the artists into two types: (1) the pioneers who, through art, expound new form concepts and techniques and (2) the painters, who employ these techniques to express ideas of a more subjective nature. In addition, there are those who are neither pioneers nor great artists; but their work, though derivative, is highly important because they use the available artistic language for social purposes.

Metzinger employed cubist techniques to represent a compilation of pertinent facts relevant to a bicycle race. He synthesized these facts into facets, symbolized by lines, planes, colors and textures, where they function as the embodiment of all that is happening at the moment (simultaneity), and as elements which decorate the picture surface (design). The pioneering ideas of Cezanne, Braque, and Picasso had finally become a new language to express the multiple experience of the mind in its reactions to the many faceted movement of forms in time and space.

CHAPTER TEN

Non-Objective Painting:

THE DYNAMICS OF SPACE

Many painters plunged wholeheartedly into the study of "what makes the picture function." In their creative research into picture analysis, they stripped the picture of all extraneous matter. Kandinsky (1866-1946) in his "Composition" (Plate XXXI), explored what would happen if the objective world was entirely excluded from the picture. He had learned from the pioneering art of Cezanne that the basic equipment of the painter consisted of lines, planes, colors and textures. Why not, said he, use these elements in their pure essence. With this in mind, he orchestrated them like musical instruments, into a symphony. They performed individually, each with a theme of its own, and yet harmonized with the whole. Within themselves they contained intrinsic beauty, a language of things of the spirit. The flat surface of the canvas served as a limitless space in which the harmony of these elements was expressed in all conceivable relationships.

In its preoccupation with the problem of space, non-objective painting contains within itself much of the "metaphysics" of the 20th century. Lines, planes and colors, as they move in space in correct juxtaposition, held together by gravitational tensions, become symbols to express the dynamics of the universe. As with Medieval art, which was philosophically abstract, the non-objective picture is constructed vertically, parallel to the picture plane, although it usually contains move-

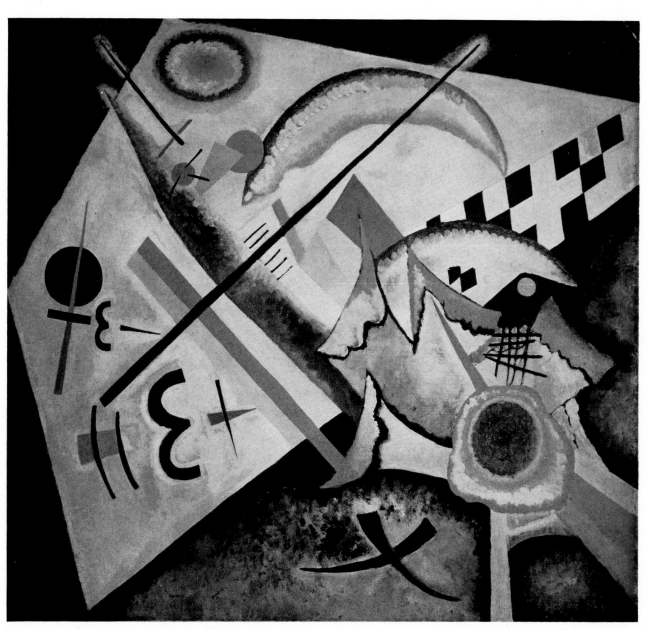

PLATE XXXI

PLATE XXXI.   COMPOSITION.   KANDINSKY

PLATE XXXII

PLATE XXXII. COMPOSITION. MONDRIAN

ment into depth. The ground plane was not employed, for the non-objective painter did not paint the factual world. Rather, his mind dwelled in universal space where lines, planes and colors moved in integrated harmony.

THE FINAL SYNTHESIS

The evolution from abstract to non-objective painting was a natural one. The tradition traced in this chapter deals with the philosophers of art, the pure painters who searched for a language compatible with contemporary thought. Many participated in this quest and contributed toward the solution. The fundamental pictorial denominator was found by Mondrian (1872-1945) who resolved its final equation.

In this process, the line and the plane were stripped of all arabesques, curves and "frivolities." They were rigidly straight and ruled, and lay parallel to each other on the picture plane. (Plate XXXII) The planes, cut out by the lines, were rectangular or square; the colors, primary (that is, unadulterated, used in their pure essence). The artist strove to reveal to the observer the beauty of fundamental mathematics. The play of the simple black line against the white square optically assumed dynamic movement. This new language of painting expressed the visual world as an experience in dynamics, the world of the 20th century.

Mondrian was the necessary culmination of the great tradition which started with Cezanne. It is sometimes contended that his art too easily resembles linoleum design or the elementary design of other household commodities. This coincidence is more than significant. The practical application of his design in no way detracts from his premise. To Mondrian the pure geometric relationship of the line to the plane established a fundamental premise from which modern design is derived. Its utilitarian application to household commodities verifies, rather than discounts his contention as to its functional properties. He established the summating equation from which the functional design in modern architecture, streamlined automobiles and interior decoration are derived. The concept of the modern world is found in his naked abstractions which, to him, were not so much pictures as expostulations of a philosophy.

Conclusion

CONTEMPORARY ART includes a recapitulation of the art of all ages. It reflects the aesthetic, philosophic and political conflict of our times. This is evident not only by the many existent schools but also by the conflicting opinions about them. In order to obtain a clearer picture of what is happening it may be well to conclude this work with a listing of the major trends in the art of today.

There are the academicians — to mention the most widely accepted group first. These painters have learned shorthand methods of perspective and form from the old masters and use them to paint non-controversial pictures, catering to popular and conventional taste.

Then there are the social commentators, propagandists and "regional" painters. They are mainly concerned with subject matter and use either perspective, or more abstract methods, for their commentary.

The surrealists have become popular through current interest in psychoanalysis. Their present leaders, Dali, Ernst and Tchelitchew, obtain their techniques from academic sources. They paint metaphors and dreams (at times culled from the textbook of Freud) with the detail and meticulous care of the 19th century salon painters. Chagall is more personal and abstract in content. Paul Klee, one of the most original painters in contemporary art, has devised an abstract poetic language to express the profundities of the inner mind. Another group in this category are the pictographers, who find inspiration in early picture writing.

The current vogue for contemporary naive paintings has resulted from the anthropological and aesthetic study of primitive and prehistoric art. Among all the arts, it is only in painting that the critics condone lack of professional skill and maturity in the name of naive charm. This demonstrates the tendency of the fashionable world to twist valid research into popular fads thereby creating a fruitful hunting ground for the opportunistic entrepreneur.

A vital group which draws largely upon Renaissance inspiration are the Mexicans Rivera, Orozco and Siquieros. They disclaim any influence of the modern school of Paris and paint gigantic murals in the grand manner, depicting the history and traditions of their country.

The abstract and non-objective painters base their art upon principles explained in the text on Braque, Picasso, Kandinsky and Mondrian. There has developed around the non-objective painters a mystical cult, which can be discounted in the study of a valid artist like Kandinsky.

Finally, come the expressionists who, under the leadership of Rouault, utilize the abstract elements of color and space for personal expression. Their forms are shaped more by their emotions than intellectual analysis. They are subjective painters whose moods and feelings dominate their work.

Opinions about these schools are as varied as the schools themselves. For instance, some people consider the modern painters as escapists, refusing to face the realities of the factual world. Others regard them as expressing a disintegrating society, with its threats of death and destruction. They look upon the work as a manifestation of the crises of our times.

However, when one learns to understand modern art and its objectives, he can find in it the opening up of new artistic frontiers. The new attempts to delve into the substance and inner meaning of man's existence are encouraging and inciting. Here is hope that the efforts of the new, enriched by the labors of the past, will succeed to unearth the means and goals of man's struggle for the good life.

The spacial evolution from antiquity to this century reflect the long road travelled by art to improve techniques and enhance creativity. The multifarious efforts—of the old, the masters and the new — are transparent in the art of today.

Notes

PAGE 26: Although a picture includes but a fraction of the cube, it is always self-contained and never fragmentary. The picture is complete in itself through a harmonious integration of the forms within its circumscribed area.

PAGE 29: When starting a picture it is preferable to begin with the nearest plane and to arrange the other forms in their proper relationship to it in space. It is difficult to start in the middle of space and to build forward from there. One must always think in terms of recession, for distances are gauged in this manner. An object is measured in distance relative to a fixed near point. In a picture this is the nearest line on the ground plane, the bottom border of the canvas.

PAGE 54: Wm. M. Ivins, Jr., in his pamphlet *On the Rationalization of Sight* (Metropolitan Museum of Art, *Papers,* Number 8, New York, 1938) describes in detail the ingenious methods employed by Alberti to discover the formula on which the theory of perspective is based.

PAGE 112: It might be mentioned that Cezanne himself was decidedly inadequate when, early in his career, he attempted a few imitations of the masters. Concerning this, it may be observed that the original artist can never fake a style adequately. He creates only within his own realm of inquiry and fails miserably when forced to move outside his predestined orbit.

PAGE 115: This analogy with the camera by no means intends to detract from the photograph's value as a work of art. Photographers within their field, have reached points of rare aesthetic achievement. We are not concerned with the relative merits of photographs and paintings, but with the contrast between camera vision and human vision.

PAGE 128: Up to the late 19th century, line, if employed at all, was primarily used to define contour, as is evident in Oriental and Medieval painting. However, as the painter became volume conscious and tried to emulate sculpture the line became obsolete, as best expressed in Goya's often quoted observation that "there are no lines in nature, since one sees only in masses." In all the great art of the past lines of action and movement were, of course, implicit, serving as an inner invisible structure which held the organization together. Line was also employed for rhythm through variated edges and rhythmic contours, as in Velasquez or Ingres.

Glossary

The technical terms listed below are fundamental to the painter's craft; they define the elements basic to all painting.

AXIS

A straight line passing through the center of a form, expressing the direction of its movement. The axis does not necessarily move parallel with the outlines of a plane. For example, in complicated forms such as the human figure, it is of the utmost importance to determine axial direction before expressing the characteristic contour. *Axes* and not *outlines* determine the relative movements of forms.

CHIAROSCURO

The technique of modeling forms through planes of light and dark created by a single external source of light.

DECORATIVE

The ornamented picture surface. Flat pattern design with emphasis on lines and planes which lie flat on the picture plane, with little or no attempt at creating an illusion of depth.

FORM

Any shape in the picture, whether volume or plane. A definite shape.

Form, in the broader meaning has been applied by artists and critics to define style or method.

LINE

The indicated distance between two points. According to their function, lines fall into the following categories; (a) they define the borders of the plane; (b) they establish distances between points; (c) they define contours; (d) they define axes; and (e) they define movements of form in space.

LINE OF MOVEMENT

The line which expresses the movement of the forms in relation to each other within the space of the picture. Controlled lines of movement make for integration and harmony, creating a *continuous path which the eye follows from object to object in the picture space.*

ORNAMENT

Elaboration of texture, pattern, design and surface quality on a plane.

PATTERN

The areas created by the design of planes on the picture surface. Pattern is a decorative element of primary consideration in the designing of a picture.

PICTURE

An idea made visible on a flat surface. It is composed of lines, planes, volumes, colors and textures. A picture may include one, several or all of the above elements. A drawing, for example, may be done in line or may be modeled in volume. Oriental art employed all these elements with the exception of volume. In the high Renaissance volume was emphasized, and line and plane subordinated, if not eliminated.

PICTURE PLANE

The surface of the picture. It is the first dimension from which all the forms recede into the space of the canvas, and upon which are recorded the images active within the picture field.

PLANE

A series of lines combined to indicate the limits of a flat surface.

PLASTICITY

The rhythmic integration of planes and volumes through movement, balanced weights and tensions. A picture is plastic when the space forms within the picture field are arranged harmoniously.

REALITY

An interpretation of nature which is compatible with concepts accepted as fact.

RHYTHM

Accent in movement at chosen intervals. Harmonious and dynamic relationship shaping the elements employed into an integrated design.

SCULPTURED FORM

This term pertains to the early Renaissance procedure of obtaining three dimensional volume by highlighting forms in the middle and gradually darkening them toward the edges.

SPACE

An arena of activity; an enclosure. The limits within which certain activities take place. In painting, space may further be described as positive space (object), and negative space (the space intervening between objects, and the space which the object occupies).

SPACE-FORM

Synonymous with volume, but considered from the viewpoint of its weight and space displacement relative to the other forms and the space of the canvas.

TENSION

The gravitational pull between planes. In abstract and non-objective art axes and lines of tension usually determine the contours of the form. In a well composed picture the forms are rhythmically balanced within the space of the canvas by implied or expressed lines of tension.

TEXTURE

Quality of surface and material employed to express smoothness. roughness, etc. Variation of textures on the picture surface add to the aesthetic meaning of the picture.

VOLUME

A sequence of planes combined to enclose a given space. Volume, in painting, is considered an elaboration of planes, and conversely, the plane is a fundamental element of volume.

This book has been set on the Linotype in 14 Pt. Baskerville. The chapter titles are Monotype 24 Pt. Deepdene Italics and the captions are Linotype Spartan Medium.

The inside stock is a No. 1 coated, No. 1C2S made by the Allied Paper Mill in Kalamazoo, Michigan, and the book is bound in Columbia Atlantic Gray Natural Smooth Finish cloth, stamped in red ink.

The engravings were made by the Kitab Engraving Co. The type was set and the book printed by The Comet Press, Inc. in New York City.